From the Biggest Casinos in Las Vegas to Brandon, Mississippi -
My Incredible Faith Journey in Finding the Promised Land - A Memoir

Betting on Faith

DAWN AMMONS

Print ISBN: 978-1-09832-018-8
eBook ISBN: 978-1-09832-019-5

Printed in the USA.

The events in this memoir are portrayed to the best of Dawn Ammons' memory, with help from her family and friends. While all the stories in this book are true, some names and identifying details have been changed to protect the privacy of the people involved.

https://www.goingallin.net

This book is dedicated to my mom, Shirley Ann Wright.

You are the strongest, most hardworking, loving woman I know. Thank you for never giving up on Max and me.

I love you,
Dawn

CONTENTS

As long as I can remember, I have been told that that one of my God-given gifts is the ability to motivate and inspire others. Whether it's because I beat self-imposed obstacles or overcame the circumstances of my childhood, I don't know. But good and bad, circumstantial or of my own creation, I *own* every aspect of my life, and *that* is critical to my success. Today, I celebrate every earned victory and every challenge I overcame because they are integral to *my life.*

In January 2017, as I sat at my desk, the urge to tell my story struck. I realized I could use those formative experiences in my early life and my career to help others chart their way through their own lives. My story is one of trauma. Of pain. Of love and loss, joy and laughter. But most importantly, my story is a testimony of faith and restoration in Jesus Christ and the grace and mercy of God, which have given me incredible hope. It's hope that I have always wanted to share with the world.

If this Kansas girl can grow up to sit in an executive office at Caesar's Palace in Las Vegas, so can you. You can do anything and everything you can imagine.

I write this book to share that *you are enough.* Your past does not determine your future. Other people do not define you. The only person who walked this Earth who can judge you is Jesus Christ. He is the only one who is perfect. As my pastors Jud Wilhite and Chip Henderson say, "It's okay to not be okay, you just don't have to stay there."

Here is to all the people watching.

Watching my triumphs.

Watching my failures.

Watching me walk away from the comfort and financial security of the casino industry and climb to find my joy in my Promised Land of Brandon, Mississippi.

"What shall we say about such wonderful things as these? **If God is for us, who can be against us?**"

(Romans 8:31)

CHAPTER 1

Putting on the Oxygen Mask

O n that warm summer day in Mississippi, the air felt thick and the sun shone bright, typical of every day in the South between April and December. That day, June 9, 2015, remains clear in my memory. It was the day I walked out. I got up and left my lucrative casino job. I was making hundreds of thousands of dollars, which is hundreds of thousands more than most Kansas girls who grow up like me ever make. The career I sacrificed almost everything to get would not keep me one more day.

Now, I would not recommend what I did next to anyone, but I did it. As a Vice President of a humongous resort, I walked out of the meeting, went to my office, and grabbed my keys and purse. As I cried, I slipped out the back door of the huge operation and headed to my car.

Once home, I typed my resignation letter.

Randy, my new husband of three months, listened as I stammered out my fears between sobs. Yes, three months. Can you imagine marrying a casino executive in Mississippi, and three months later she leaves her job? He must have thought, "We are *not* in Vegas anymore. Those high-paying entertainment jobs are not found every day here!" He has never complained once or second guessed my choice, even to this day. My husband turned out to be the most supportive man I could ask for.

My doctor, my neurologist, my OB/GYN, and my counselor said I needed to leave the job for my health, which had grown horrible beyond measure. My stomach churned, perpetually upset. I gained weight, developed stress headaches, and succumbed to every infection. I became quickly agitated with others, including my family, and lived in a heightened state of anxiety. None of this happened in a vacuum. While I struggled, I worried about the impact I had on the people around me.

But before I could worry about them, I had to strap the "oxygen mask" on myself first.

To move on with my life, I needed to put on my "big-girl panties" and keep going. After all, this had been my M.O. since I was a little girl. Chugging along was all I'd ever known.

CHAPTER 2

There's No Place Like Home

H utchinson, Kansas. My hometown. Hutchinson is nestled in the near dead center of our beautiful country. Surrounded by wheat fields, it is a town of yesteryear. Founded in the 1870s with the arrival of the Santa Fe Railway, it's now a sweet little city of 40,000 people. Flying over Hutch, you can watch the city unfold like a massive checkerboard in the middle of the plains. A few trees spatter the blocks, and grain elevators edge the Southern part of town.

Growing up, I felt Hutch embodied the perfect town to be from. Since we rarely traveled, I thought it was a sprawling city. Driving south on Main Street as a child, the scent of baking bread at Betts Bakery wafted in through the car windows. The sweet smell permeated downtown. Kids went to one of three high schools: the big public high school, which I graduated from, and two smaller private schools.

I sensed from a young age that my family didn't have much money, and nowhere was that clearer than where we shopped. I wished I could buy from the beautiful stores like Pegues, Wiley's, and Terry Bloskey's, where the girls from money bought their Izods, Wiggle Jeans, and Calvin Kleins.

Midwestern retail stores like Gibson's and ALCO and the Ben Franklin five-and-dime were part of the fabric of my family's weekends; my mother would pull me and my brother along on trips to window-shop and occasionally buy something. I will never forget how in fifth grade I got one heck of a spanking in ALCO after I begged for fashionable boots: pleather knee boots that zipped up the side. It didn't matter that they didn't sell any that would zip over my chunky calves. We couldn't afford them anyway! But I told my mother I *needed* them to fit in with the rich girls at school. My little brother

Max looked on while I cried in the middle of the store, and, learning from my mistakes, told my mom that plain red rubber boots sounded great.

My home kept me busy with city pools, a skating rink, a zoo with a few llamas, and eventually a small water park outside town. The state penitentiary bordered the south side of town, and Prairie Dunes Country Club, which gave Hutchinson a name in the world of golfing, bordered the east.

There were some very unique aspects to Hutchinson, too. We had the Kansas Cosmosphere, named "one of the first affiliates of the Smithsonian Institution," and Strataca, the Kansas Underground Salt Museum located 650 feet below the Earth's surface. Underground Vaults and Storage, which stores many famous movies such as "Gone with the Wind" and "Ben-Hur," was right outside town, too. Hutchinson also hosts the Kansas State Fair each year, the NJCAA National Basketball Tournament, and the old Fox Theatre. I grew up a proud Hutchinson High School Salthawk.

In the 1970s, families flocked to our safe little world in Kansas. My brother Max and I rode bikes all day in the summer, sunup to sundown. We swam at the city swimming pools from open until close, eating as many neon orange Chick-o-Sticks, RazzApple Fun Dips, and striped bags of popcorn as we had change to buy. During the winter, we roller-skated our weekends away at the Whirls of Fun skating rink on North Lorraine.

My family took a couple vacations within the Midwest when my brother and I were still little. We traveled to Mount Rushmore by way of Bedrock City—a Flintstones-themed campground in South Dakota—and to the Royal Gorge Canyon in Colorado. And a few times a year, we packed into whatever car we owned and made the daylong trek to Nebraska, where my parents were both born and raised—my mother in Elm Creek and my father in Alliance. All our family lived in Nebraska except the four of us. My childhood was dotted with days spent in the back of a beat-up blue two-door Ford Galaxy or our old white police car, windows rolled down, my brother and I laying on the floor or poking our heads out to peer at the endless sky.

Mom, Max, and I still talk about the day Dad popped. Once, when we were driving down I-80 in Nebraska, my brother had pushed him too far. When Max got bored on the long drives, he would thump Dad on the back of his bald head and taunt me, thinking the adults seated up front were too far to punish him. That day, Dad warned him, "If you don't stop it, I am going to pull the car over and whip you."

Max responded: "Pull the car over and whip me."

It happened in slow motion. Dad swerved the car over on I-80 and told Max to get out. He didn't bother to open his door but pulled Max out through the driver's side window and spanked him quiet. That boy did not let out a peep for the rest of the trip.

Max didn't learn from this beating. He continued to push Mom and Dad's limits and received years more of spankings. I learned quickly and was blessed with only a couple of "life-altering experiences."

Since I left Kansas, most of the people I meet in my travels never encountered a Kansan, and their only pop culture reference is Dorothy from *The Wizard of Oz*. From the outside, we looked like so many of our neighbors and friends, the typical Kansan family of the 1970s. My mother was a housewife. My dad worked at Cessna, the small hydraulic manufacturer and one of the largest businesses in town.

My father was a handsome, brilliant, and witty man. His friends joked if anyone needed to "phone a friend" for the game show *Who Wants to Be a Millionaire*, they ought to call my dad.

Dad left Alliance, Nebraska, after high school in the 1960s and headed to Hanover, New Hampshire to attend Dartmouth. In pictures, he stands with his little beanie on his head beside his dad, Max E. Wright. My grandpa, a man of few smiles, couldn't hide how proud he felt in those photos. *Animal House* stories filled my dad's college years. He hitchhiked to and from Nebraska to get home on holiday breaks.

After Dad graduated from Dartmouth, he headed off to the Army. Why he went into the armed forces I don't know; he wasn't drafted. Sadly, I never really got to talk to him about serving. He told us a few stories about how he learned *not* to tell drill instructors he graduated from college (and Ivy League, no less). His first proud moment talking about Dartmouth led him to horrible assignments which taught him to keep his mouth shut.

Dad's key takeaway from those years was, "Don't be first and don't be last." And be quiet.

In 1966, my parents met at the Nebraska State Fair in Lincoln through a mutual friend. After his time in the Army, he got a job with DuPont, which was a big deal in the 1960s. My parents went on rides together and played carnival games. Before long, they were dating seriously. Soon, a hiring manager at Cessna wrote Dad and asked him to look at a job in Hutchinson, Kansas. Even though they were not yet married, the two of them loaded up her old Ford and drove to look at the job. A few months later, Dad and Mom got married in Elm Creek, Nebraska, at the First Christian Church before packing up their bags to move south to Kansas.

Like millions of others in this world, my dad—this crazy intelligent, handsome, and funny man—had a disease that overtook his life. My dad was an alcoholic. A functioning alcoholic, for decades actually. He drank cheap vodka and Schlitz. His struggle with drinking colored most memories of home.

As a young child, my mom and I followed a nighttime routine that certainly differed from most of my friends. Mom would get me in the car and drive into town, down to East 4th. Half-asleep in the cool night air, the sounds of the gravel parking lot crunching woke me up as my mom drove us up to my dad's favorite dive: Nashville South. There, we usually found my dad, too drunk to drive, and brought him back home. When I wasn't picking up my father late at night, I was at the bar with him. During our trips to Nashville South, we always parked so we could walk in the back door. Eating pickles and corn nuts while my dad drank, I sat at the bar and listened to the juke box. The fact that we were at a bar didn't really matter; I just loved spending time next to him.

Every Saturday morning while Max and I watched *Schoolhouse Rock*, my dad read the newspaper and had a drink. On Sunday mornings, the scene (Dad, newspaper, drink) remained the same, but Max and I watched *Davey and Goliath*, our televised church of the '70s. Dad managed to still be responsible at work, showing up every morning and being present for his coworkers and their needs. But he was not always around for my brother and me when we were young.

I distinctly remember one weekend morning, Dad told my brother, who was in elementary school at the time, that he would take him to the rodeo.

Max got all ready. He pulled his brown straw cowboy hat low on his forehead and pushed his blue jeans down into his little cowboy boots. Max bounced onto the couch and sat. And then laid down. And waited. I watched from a distance, sad, knowing my drunk dad had probably already forgotten. He was not going to take Max to the rodeo. After the morning passed, Mom made an excuse for Dad, and the three of us continued on as usual. To this day, Max remembers. We all remember.

As the older sister, I was better at steeling myself against the disappointment I felt when my dad let us down. Then came my bicycle accident in sixth grade. On a warm, sunny Kansas day, some of my friends and I were riding bicycles a few blocks away from home. We did donuts on our bikes in the parking lot at Dillon's grocery store on 13th and Main. Too many of us wound up whizzing around each other in one corner of the lot, and my bicycle and Larry Stephen's bicycle collided. Our bicycles went flying, and Larry and I flipped over our handlebars and flew through the air. In the flurry of limbs and wheels, I landed face up on the pavement with a gash an inch-long and over an inch deep in my right thigh, so deep that everything that was supposed to be inside my leg came out. There were kids running and screaming everywhere. One of my friends ran inside in a frenzy, and an older kid who had been inside sacking groceries came out and put his white apron over me. He told me everything was going to be okay and stayed with me, holding my hand. Someone called an ambulance, and my friends pedaled off to tell my parents.

My throbbing leg and the crash in front of all my friends were not the worst parts of my day. It was my dad showing up drunk to impart his wound-treating "knowledge" on everyone, EMTs and all. Once again, my superhero mom jumped in to smooth over my dad's drunken scene. Shirley had presence. She unfolded her sturdy, 5'9" frame from the car, and her booming voice carried across the parking lot. When my mom meant business, she let everyone know. Dad caused trouble, yes, but she all but put him in timeout and took over. Off I went to the hospital with mom riding shotgun. My leg was going to be okay.

The stitches I received that day, both internal and external, left a scar still vivid today at 51. Now and then, while stretching on the floor after a gym class, I catch ladies glancing at and then looking away from my leg. Some ask what happened. Though I tell them about my bicycle wreck, I don't tell them of the physical and emotional pain of the day when I couldn't to conceal the family turbulence I otherwise tried so diligently to hide.

Like many children of alcoholics, especially firstborn, I prioritized keeping the chaos hidden. Children of alcoholics learn to cover the elephant in the room. At school, I primarily focused on achieving in the classroom and bringing home amazing grades. In sixth grade, the teacher had to get a new book for me because I excelled out of the top reading group. "Just keep swimming," as Dory from *Finding Nemo* would say. Tasking myself with keeping normalcy in our lives, I tried to make it appear the Wright family had it all together. Above all else, I wanted to make my mom and dad proud. I hoped if he saw how hard I studied, how good I was, Dad might stop drinking.

Once I moved into fifth and sixth grade, Dad's drinking got worse. Drunk or sober, he never yelled. He sat in the dining room with his vodka, headphones on, listening to Handel's "Messiah," Herb Albert & the Tijuana Brass, The Mamas and The Papas, The Statler Brothers, Johnny Cash, and Elvis. My mom, the most hard-working, loving woman I know, kept the three-ring circus going all without a word of complaint to me or my brother. Christmases, summers, school years came and went.

All through this time, Mom kept watch over our family money. She sat at the dining room table with scattered bills and pieces of paper. In her notebook, she listed each bill and the amount due. While we never had much money, it became clear she had less and less to pay the bills. She crossed off the amount as soon as she put the check in the mailbox. I knew my dad worked a great job, but it seemed things were tight. Tighter than I would expect for his position. Now I know why. The money did not always make it home. Years later, Mom told me Dad wrote checks directly to liquor stores and Nashville South, and she didn't know until after the fact. She stashed some money so we had enough to buy food and pay the bills and the $200 house note. Paying off the house meant everything to her. To this day my mother will not say anything specifically bad about Dad. Only, "You know your father," and, "We made it. Somehow."

Then one day in eighth grade, my dad was gone. Days went by with no sign of him. My mother told Max and me that Dad was with his brother, my Uncle Frank, in Nebraska and would be gone for a while. I could see the hurt and fear in my mother's eyes and knew that "a while" meant more than a week. Few people knew he'd left home. I kept on "doing the dance" at school and with my friends.

After a few days, my mom sat and talked with Max and me. My father had checked into treatment in Valley Hope in O'Neill, Nebraska. His brother Frank, a recovered alcoholic, had taken him there to save his life. Inside, I felt so relieved. What treatment in rehab entailed confused me, but I started to hope my dad would get well and come home. Maybe everything would be normal. So, my mother, brother, and I kept going.

Throughout this time, and the rest of my childhood, my mother's family in Nebraska gave us sturdy, unwavering support. Mom always turned to her sisters Judy, Tresa, and Darlene for support. My aunts and their families had as little money as we did, but they shared a crazy amount of love with us. From my aunts, uncles, and cousins, I learned that love and happiness have not a thing to do with money.

Aunt Judy, Mom's youngest sister, was her best friend and my second mom. Mom talked to her on the phone daily, and she sent Mom money to help buy our school clothes. What she lacked in age and height (unlike my mom, she stood about 5'0" tall), she made up in fight. A feisty redhead, she lived as tough as they made them.

She lived in a small, white house on the corner of a gravel road in the wee little town of Pleasanton, Nebraska. Pleasanton, population: 300, sits on the South Loop River just north of Kearney. Pictures from her 1973 wedding to my Uncle Jack show him in his army uniform, Aunt Judy with her bouffant hair, and me licking the champagne glass at the age of 5. (Note to self: I should have stopped then.) She never had it easy. My uncle was a farmer, and he worked hard on his family farm outside Pleasanton. At the end of long days on the farm, he went down to the "the office," the local bar. He didn't spend much time home, and my aunt always seemed a little frustrated with everyone, even me at times, close as we were. She also bore the pain of losing their only child, Carla Jo, who was stillborn the day after Christmas in 1976.

When I visited as a child and spent summers with them as a teen, life out on the farm enthralled me. While Uncle Jack set pivots and worked in the fields, I looked on, mesmerized. It became clear I wasn't cut out for farm work: those fat, scary pigs…those sows were *mean*. But those pigs didn't intimidate Uncle Jack's mom, Dorothy, one bit. I feared her. She was such a wiry, knotted woman, aged by the sun, and I figured if she could handle pigs with a shovel, I ought to stay in check around her. The first time I saw a head come off a chicken (and every time the dreaded chicken picker rolled around), I went screaming for the house. As much as Hutchinson was *not* a big city, I *was* a city girl.

Aunt Judy left this earth too early. In November 2007, she passed away from complications due to the anti-obesity treatment Fen-Phen, which the FDA later took off the market because it caused heart attacks in the women who took it. I was blessed to be in the hospital room with Mom, Aunt Darlene, and Uncle Jack when she took her last breath. Besides teaching me how to mow a huge lawn with a push mower, Aunt Judy gave me her time—something Mom didn't always have the luxury to do. I will always feel grateful for the hours we passed canning, sewing, cooking, doing ceramics, latch hooking, and knitting. I was bad at all of it and my Aunt Judy knew that. I was blessed the most with the time she spent with me. And I am most grateful for her friendship with Mom and the love she shared with us.

Mom's oldest sister, Darlene, and her husband, Vic, owned another farm outside Pleasanton that reminded me of Auntie Em's in *The Wizard of Oz*. A cute little farmhouse, an outside cellar, a barn, and a chicken hut stood neatly together on their swatch of land. We spent many holidays crammed around the worn wooden table in their kitchen, surrounded by the collection of back scratchers which hung on the wall. As years went by and everyone started adding spouses and children to the Christmas table, the kitchen and living room overflowed with relatives. But we still had room for All-Star wrestling.

My aunts' homes in Nebraska were our safe spaces. This family hurt when we hurt. To me, driving to Pleasanton or Elm Creek from Hutchinson was alternately an escape and a grand vacation—even though we sometimes only had enough money for gas and a truck-stop meal.

After about a month of life without him, Dad came home. The change in his personality shocked me. While he had always been subdued, he was now quiet and serious, reflective and present. Before rehab, my dad had been witty, like my brother. But when he came home, he appeared more humble than anything.

He went back to work and started to go to AA meetings.

In the beginning, I knew little about what the "AA way of life" entailed. He went to meetings every day in a little old house that no longer stood quite straight. Someone had plastered posters across every wall. People smoked everywhere and chatted until the meeting started. The aroma of cigarettes and coffee permeated the front room. After meetings, Dad drank coffee with others in the group. Over time, I could tell he grew to respect and love the friends he made there. It took me a while to meet them, and though I never knew their full names, they profoundly affected my family's life. These first-name friends of my father were always calm and soothing, full of peace and joy. It made me happy inside that Dad hung out with them. AA became a peaceful and safe way of life for us. I would come to know Dad's sponsor Tom much better than I ever expected.

After Dad got involved in AA, we started to go as a family to Park Place Christian Church, and Dad and Mom became involved in my youth group. I will never forget how I beamed when they volunteered together to bring dinner one night for our youth group. To this day, I can picture Mom, Dad, and myself standing in the church kitchen preparing the meal. The memory of the three of us together, volunteering, is bittersweet. I felt valued, and I know my mom's heart was filled by being with her husband and daughter after years of pain. I was so happy for this sweet moment of togetherness.

But it all changed. My mother began crying again. She cried at home and during sermons. I felt so lost. Life changed into something new, silent, and somber. I remember the day well, when my parents sat Max and me down in the living room of 116 West 16th street and said they were separating. I sat there in the room beside myself. The living room with floor-to-ceiling paneling and orange shag carpet was closing in on me.

"Wait. What? Dad isn't drinking. Why is he getting an apartment?"

But my mother just kept crying, and they divorced for reasons she would never share. Mom kept as much as she could away from me and Max regarding the relationship between her and Dad. He didn't drink anymore, but something changed between them that couldn't be fixed.

Mom was (and is) a woman of integrity, kindness, and strength.

I hated my dad. I didn't understand their separation or its impact on me, and I fumed. I didn't want to see his new apartment. I didn't want to go to auctions with his AA friends to get furniture. I wanted our life back, and I wanted Mom to quit crying.

But I never got that part of my childhood back.

Looking back now—after decades of sermons, counselors, books, and AA meetings of my own—I can see that this time in my life created the young girl who begged for belonging, acceptance, and not to be abandoned by the man she respected the most.

CHAPTER 3

Scrappy is Old School for Innovative

After the divorce, Mom went to work. Dad always paid child support, but it did not pay the bills. Though she took on two or three jobs at a time and rarely spent time at home, she never complained.

Mom served lunches at our grade school, Roosevelt, a few houses away; worked at a laundry mat for years washing and folding other people's clothes; babysat; and worked on the assembly line at Cessna. Money stressors eased up a bit when she was there, but Cessna laid her off after only a few years.

Eventually, Mom worked at the Midwestern ice cream chain Braum's serving cones and working the drive-thru. She found her spot when she moved to the grocery area and took pride in keeping her bread, ice cream, and frozen food areas stocked and neat. Braum's, like many small-town restaurants, had regulars who came in for coffee and fellowship in the mornings, and Mom loved visiting them while she worked. Not only did she talk about work all the time, but she showed off her awards for safety and customer service. This still makes me giggle.

Middle school came and went. I grew up fast because I tried to cover for my family's craziness and still be a kid. With my father trying to put together a new life for himself and my mother working overtime to keep us in our house, I moved into the role of trying to help parent my little brother.

For those people who know my brother Max Wright, he is one in a million. Like me, Max was scrappy and full of "piss and vinegar." I wish I could say it nicer, but it is the truth. "Pee" is not the right word to describe Max.

Max is five years younger than me and doesn't know a stranger. As a child, he had messy blonde hair and glasses. He frequently wore too-short Toughskin jeans and worn-out tennis shoes. A boy in every possible way, he buried all our utensils in the dirt beside the house, rode his bike until he popped every tube Dad had, roller-skated, swam, wrestled, and played football from the moment he could walk. Football was his love. He played basketball, too. Though he could dribble like a beast, he shot the ball like a shot put. He never ever slowed down. Max got his desk moved by teachers every year because he loved to talk and, quite frankly, he enjoyed entertaining the class. I vividly remember the day I walked by his second grade classroom and had to take a double-take. There was Max Geoffrey Wright sitting at his desk, now fully planted in the hallway. We made eye contact and he shook his little head. I know what he was telling me: *Don't tell Mom and Dad, Dawn.* Instead, I heard: *Sprint home as fast as you can to tell Mom and Dad.* And that's just what I did. I sprinted the whole block home before Max and "reported my findings." It did not stop there. In fourth grade, Mrs. Eusen moved his and a friend's desk to the back of the room, facing the wall. When my parents saw this at the parent-teacher conference, Max, ever quick on his feet, said, "Mrs. Eusen did not want us to rub off on other kids."

Max's popularity grew through high school, and he ended up becoming the captain of the football team and homecoming king. He loved the girls, and the girls loved him. Max always had tons of friends because he is kind, compassionate, and funny. And the same holds true today.

We did not always see eye to eye. I thought he and his friends were gross, smelly, and obnoxious. They in turn snubbed their noses at me, the nerdy older sister who tried to keep order in our orderless world.

As much as a high school student and a grade school student can love each other, we did not. Max and I fought about everything. I won most of our physical altercations for two reasons. One, I outweighed him (being chubby helped in this area) and two, Dad did not let him hit girls, including his sister. Though I loved him and would do anything to help raise him, we drove each other crazy. Sometimes a good "thump" made us both feel better, until the day Max blew a gasket.

Max went outside to get the mail, the newspaper, or something but rather than get dressed, he went outside without a shirt and only his underwear on. He was still young, in middle school, but being five years older, I needed someone in this crazy world to believe I was boss. And quite frankly I wanted a laugh. So, I locked the screen door and "politely" told him to stand on his head. I "politely" told him if he stood on his head, I would let him back in.

After we traded a few loud obscenities, Max kept yelling "Let me in." I yelled back, "Stand on your head." After a few minutes, I saw his refusal to stand on his head was serious. I walked away with the screen door locked and Max standing on the front porch of 116 West 16th in his underwear.

I walked back into our bathroom—the only bathroom in the house for our whole family—and closed the folding door. In this tiny room, I could sit on the toilet, wash my hands, and turn on the bathtub all at once. I went back to curling my hair.

Before I knew it, I heard a huge crash outside and in came Max Wright in his underwear, and he was *scary* (even for a little kid). His face burned bright red and his blue eyes bulged out of his head. He wrenched the folding door open with his little hands and I tried to pull it shut, but he held tight.

I saw my life flash in front of my eyes. I brandished my only defense, the curling iron.

"Max, if you don't stop, I am going to burn you," I said. "Burn me," he screamed. So I reached out and lunged toward him with the iron as he charged at me with his fists. I burned him with the barrel, a critical error on my part. He became insane, incensed by the pain. We exchanged a few punches and I tried to get out of the tiny bathroom before it became the location of my death. In the process of fighting my way out, Max tore the door off the hinges. I *knew* I was dead.

I ran a few steps to the kitchen and grabbed a fork to defend myself.

"Fork me!" he shouted.

I knew better than to fork him, so I pushed past him and ran out the front door, noticing as I went the broken screen door hung from its hinges. I flew out the door and tripped down the street, crying and telling anyone who would listen that Max—my tiny, blue-eyed, grade school brother—was trying to kill me. I ran down to the neighbors till I knew I was safe.

Brad Swisher from next door and the "other Wrights" (Keith and Judy down the street, of no relation to us) came out and brought me in. Together, Keith, Brad, Judy, and I made the trip back down to my house to see the damage and assess the situation. And there Max stood, clothed this time, brandishing a hammer in his tiny fist. Brad and the Wrights thought he had come at me with a hammer. Max explained the story—which matched up with mine—and told them he had the hammer to fix the screen door and bathroom door before Mom got home. Everyone took a deep breath, relieved. Myself included!

That was the last day we ever got into a physical altercation. No more thumps on the head or wrestling matches, ever. We still had disagreements but never fought that way again. Max did not get in trouble with Dad, and Mom said the three weeks that followed were the quietest ever at 116 West 16th.

Max and I were complete opposites. I did not like that he listened to KISS and blasted hard rock. I loved John Denver, Loverboy, and the *Grease* soundtrack. It bothered me that he was covered in layers of grime, and that he and his friends, Buddha, Griff, Brian, Travis, and Lucas, were "gross." (Please note, all these men are first-rate men today: hardworking and successful with beautiful families. But at the time, they were gross.) Max scoffed at the fact that I was a dork and unpopular.

Though that kid could frustrate me more than anyone in the world, no one could say a bad thing about Max Wright in my presence. I spent much of my time growing up trying to help provide for him and to shield him for the craziness in our house. When Mom was not home (which was most of the time), I also helped make sure Max had dinner. The food wasn't good or anything, but he ate. I made mac and cheese, Braunschweiger liverwurst sandwiches, and Hamburger Helper. I tried to make some "Mom-type" foods—her specialty: scrambled eggs and hot dogs—but usually we reverted to sandwiches, Shasta pop, and sour cream and onion chips. But when Mom came home and made her specialty, Max's friends loved it. To this day, they comment on his Facebook posts about her food. Personally, I still cannot eat a hot dog.

Beside dinners, I made sure that when Max had a school project or Cub Scout event, he was covered. I didn't want the guy to look or feel bad in front of his friends and their parents. Dad and Max did the Pinewood Derby. Dad, who always wanted to turn things into engineering projects, made sure their car ran. (Unfortunately, one year, the only way to gain any speed down the track was to run it backwards.) Dad, like me, was crazy book smart but sometimes not so street smart. Or so I have been told.

Outside of the derby, I took care of most school and extracurricular projects. I took pride in being the sister who baked cakes at the annual Cub Scout cake auction. Max Wright won the award for the highest-bid cake two years in a row, even though his cake was shown up by those of his friends, which were made by their mothers, grandmothers, aunts, or professional bakeries. Max won because every parent could tell the two of us made it. Clearly! One year we made Pac-Man out of a yellow circle cake with a piece cut out for a mouth and a blue eye. The next, we iced a rectangle-shaped basketball court with court markings and free-throw lines. The one problem with this particular cake was that it fell, and we remade one half of completely from frosting. Regardless, Max and I cheerfully walked two blocks from our house to Trinity United Methodist Church with his cake in hand to the auctions. He always proudly placed his cakes on the table, and we sat in the audience. Each year, I watched Max's face as parents would outbid each other for his cakes. Those parents (and I) knew exactly what they were doing, but Max was simply proud.

••

Dad remarried soon after the divorce. I never said anything about the timing, but deep in my heart I knew.

Max and I shied away from their house in the beginning. I busied myself with cross-country and swim team, but Max had to go over after school and for dinner. Soon I went too because I missed my father, and I loved him a lot. But I also hurt because I knew he was building a new life with his new wife. Max and I spent some Saturdays over there watching football or working with my dad in his office. His new wife had two children, and Max and I were very different from them. I knew one thing for sure, though. My dad loved his new wife Dee, and I did not know how I felt about that.

One evening in high school, Dad and I had "The Confrontation." My brother and I made trips over to my dad and Dee's for dinner each week. Together they turned their little ranch-style house into a beautiful home.

Inside, it was a bit trendy. A huge, plush, beige couch, which fit the whole family, took up much of the living room. One night, we sat in the living room among Dee's plants. Something about being in his *new* home with his *new* furniture and *new* wife made me tighten up. Now he wanted to start fresh? And that was supposed to erase the years of his absence and drinking? My throat tightened up, and I popped a socket.

"For how many years have you been missing? Absent? Are you kidding me? Now you wanna be super dad? Forget it." I let loose—sobbing and screaming at him.

My dad directed me across the living room and into the main bathroom, so we had privacy from Max, Dee, and her son. I continued to cry and yell at him. My dad just blinked back. He was 5'10", bald and wore glasses, and even when he did drink, he was mostly quiet. He never cut an imposing figure.

I shouted at him. "You can't expect things to be fine in one day."

My dad responded calmly.

"Ding," his pet name for me, "I can't change the past. I wish I could. I just know I want to make today right." Dad was working the AA steps: trying to make amends by *living* amends. For many children of alcoholics, myself included, "sorry" stops meaning anything when it's followed up by more broken promises, mistakes, and let-downs. My dad tried to say he could only live that day as the best possible man, father, and husband he could be. He was calm when he explained this to me, and when we got done, a sense of relief washed over me. I understood him, and I'd finally said what I'd wanted to say. But I also felt angry and exhausted.

I looked at him.

"I just don't know," I said. I walked out of the bathroom. "Come on Max. We're leaving." My brother and I were our own posse, and he followed me out without questioning me. When we got in the car to drive the ten minutes back to Mom's, Max turned to me. "What was that?"

"Nothing," I said. "I don't know." But I felt better. My dad recognized I was entitled to being upset, sad, and hurt. He knew I needed to say my piece, and he needed to listen. That was part of the process. Over the next few days, I felt a bit sorry and remorseful that I yelled at him. In those days, I didn't cut him any slack.

Day by day…one day at a time, my relationship with my Dad got better. He consistently showed up when he said he would for both me and Max. He came to my cross-country meets and Max's football games, decked out in his Hutchinson High School Salt Hawk sweatshirts and shirts at every game, home or away. Dad engaged in our lives, and we knew he loved us. He wanted to do the right thing as a dad, husband, stepdad, friend, and boss.

But trust is broken overnight and earned over time. Though he slowly started to prove himself, I waited for the other shoe to drop—for him to leave or outright disappear. Though not a healthy way to think, I was a teenager and my family didn't have the money for me to go talk to someone.

He wanted to be a good dad. I know that. He wanted a do-over and the chance to prove himself, but I didn't feel ready for that yet. Yes, he was my hero, but I felt so confused and hurt. He had betrayed and abandoned me. Those feelings of betrayal and abandonment would stay with me for a couple of decades. If I had known then what I know now, I would have talked to a Christian counselor *way* earlier and saved myself and others years of pain.

Dad now approached life with one philosophy: "One Day at A Time," a principle from Alcoholics Anonymous. All he could do was be his best and work on his sobriety, each day. Max and I went with that, and it was good for us because it made sense. But my dad's disease would rear its ugly head again.

I had started gaining weight during the latter part of grade school, and gained a lot more during middle school and early high school. Food became my way to cope with my dad's drinking, his treatment, separation, divorce, and the new man he became in his sobriety. I ate to handle everything. My freshman high school picture is nowhere to be found because I tore up every copy. I had square hair and awkward, thick glasses which swallowed my face. Even just thinking about the picture brings back such pain. It still haunts me to recall how tough my life was then. That little girl hurt; I desired to be "normal" and fit in, but maintaining my show of normalcy became harder. As I gained weight, girls at school started bullying me. They snickered at me in the hallways, letting me know I didn't look "cool" in my Olivia Newton-John headband. I couldn't afford Calvin Klein jeans, Izods, or a meal at Pegues downtown like the rich girls could, and they let me know the "in" crowd was no place for me.

In eighth grade, I tried out for basketball. Not only did I *not* make the team, but the head coach offered me a babysitting job for his kids instead. It can't get any worse than that, but I did it. Holy embarrassing.

By the time I got to ninth grade, I was tired of being fat, tired of being different, "sick and tired of being sick and tired." It was time to do something about it.

My three friends were excellent swimmers on our school team: Laura Ewy, Lora Menze, and Kathy Zink. After they talked me into it, I signed up for the team. Laura, Lora, and Kathy were exceptionally talented. They had been swimming for years. I was not good, at all. Sure, my mom took me every summer to Red Cross swim lessons, but swimming 100 yards and doing a flip turn? Not on your life.

I was going to try it. I planned to show up and practice, every single day. Even if I swam in the slow lane, I would push myself to show up and work. We started with freestyle. Our coach, Glee Jewel, did not give up on me. Many days at practice, she and I practiced flip turns in the shallow end. My swim team season consisted of pushing through arduous practices and surviving meets. I couldn't do the fly at all. Back stroke, which required I do my pulls and then count from the flags to the wall for a flip turn, took a lot out of me. That was going to be a hard no. In meets, Coach Jewel put me in freestyle.

It didn't matter how fast I could swim, or which strokes I mastered. This was my first real introduction to exercise, and swimming gave me something healthy to focus on outside home. The first time I worked hard at something, I got results. I carried this lesson with me through my career and adult life.

Swim team saved my life.

But while the exercise became a healthy way for me to cope with my stress at home, I fell into another not-so-healthy coping mechanism. Concerned about my appearance—and seeing the way my body and weight changed when I started exercising—I focused on eating less. Way less. My meals weren't enough to give me the energy I needed. Since I couldn't ask Mom to buy more expensive, healthy food, I ate less. For months, I ate the same three meals every day: Melba toast and orange juice for breakfast and dinner and salad with lemon for lunch. That was it.

This diet was wrong for so many reasons. But I know now I ate like this because I could control something. At the time, I thought this diet was healthy and nutritious; after all, I got results. But swim team became harder because I quickly grew tired and lethargic. So, I was bad *and* had no energy. But, because of Laura, Lora, and Kathy, I didn't give up. They would never let me. My swimsuit got too baggy, and my goal became to make it through the season, so we didn't have to buy another one. Swim team came and went that spring of 1983.

And though my eating was unhealthy, the exercise made me happier and more confident. On the outside, most people said I *always* was a happy and energetic kid. But for the first time, I started to feel like I was in control. Living a happy life was entirely up to me, not my circumstances or the people around me. The ebb and flow of my home life was not for me to solve, nor was the way middle school or high school girls treated me, or if a boy liked me. I knew my heart was good, and started to see I was a funny, smart, hard-working girl.

That summer, Laura and Lora invited me to start running with them. I got a pair of Nike Pegasus tennis shoes and hit the streets. I ran all over the streets of Hutchinson where there were flat roads for days. The hotter it was outside, the more I liked the run. In August, I signed up for cross-country at school, starting my life-long love of running.

Never in a million years did my parents think I would love running. I was the fat girl who rode a skateboard with a motorcycle helmet (a walk-a-thon prize) strapped on. But I loved running! It put my mind into a happy, blissful state. I could run all over Hutch and forget about my troubles at home and school.

As my summer of running came to a close, I prepared to go back to school and face the bullies with my newfound sense of confidence. Still, I was nervous.

On the first day of school my sophomore year, 1983, I was standing outside in the Quad, when Eric Nelson, my neighbor and an upperclassman, walked up to me. Eric was popular, a cute guy in the in-crowd. While I knew he had to know me—I lived around the corner and across the street, and we had mutual friends—we had only spoken a handful of times. To him, I probably was just the chubby little neighbor girl riding her skateboard with the motorcycle helmet.

Eric walked up to me and asked if I was Dawn Wright. I froze. Inside, I was ecstatic. Someone noticed me? A cute, upperclassman who could play the drums like Peter Chris in KISS noticed ME! Of course, I smiled and said yes, it was me, Dawn. Eric said he didn't recognize me.

There I stood that first day of school weighing 95 lbs. Someone noticed me! I was not invisible.

This is when I started to notice that, sadly, size and weight mattered to people. People treated me differently when I was thin. They held doors open and listened to me when I talked. They laughed when I laughed and taunted me less. They noticed me. In my mind, I could control how people treated me merely by controlling what I put in my mouth. In my high school years, I was teetering between depending on the acknowledgment, appreciation, and value placed on me by the world and being able to value and love myself. It would take some years before I believed in myself.

I enjoyed high school. My sophomore year I joined the cross-country team with Lora and Laura, and that made all the difference in the world to my psyche and my heart. Our first meet was somewhere outside Wichita. The course wound its way through brown fields and over hills dotted with a few trees. As this was my very first cross-country race, I had no expectations. I got up on the line spray painted across the field with dozens of girls from our league and my coach. Coach George was a small, compact man, but he had huge life and energy for us kids whether or not we won.

The gun shot sounded, and I knew to run as fast as I could for two miles. Just. Run. Fast. And that is *exactly* what I did. All I remember is running in a field for a few minutes. Back then we didn't have all the technology to tell us our pace, our heart rate, calories burned etc. Someone yelled times at the one-mile marker, and before I knew it, I finished. At the finish line, Coach George was beaming, jumping up and down as I crossed. He was so proud of me.

At the end of the meet, I medaled! Me! Dawn Wright, who could not ride a skateboard without getting winded a year before, won a medal! I was one of the top 25 women to cross the line—and at my first meet. Coach George hugged me, and I was introduced to the tender feeling of winning.

Just two years before I was overweight and depressed. How did it happen? I believed in myself enough to suit up, stop binge eating, and start working out by first swimming and then running. And the crazy thing is I thought that was pretty easy.

I won that race because I *got out of my own way*. I was not in my own head for that one race. I had no expectations for a two-mile race, so *I just ran*. I didn't think about the hills, the heat, the competition, or if my shoelaces were tied tight enough. And I won.

It took me years to look back on this day and think about what it said about my drive. On a run one day some 30+ years later, I jogged the mile warm-up lap I have mapped out in my subdivision. It was a hot, humid Mississippi summer day, and I was thinking over a few things, when my mind turned back to the day of that first race.

That day in cross-country my sophomore year, I medaled because I did not play some story forward in my head about running two miles, or think about how hot it was, or how it was my first meet, or that I didn't have the best running shoes, or, or, or...

I ran and enjoyed myself.

I had no fear.

I trained hard, and I didn't worry about anyone else and their opinion of me, or if they ran faster than me. I realized all my successes in this world—my career, my journey to health, the races run, and the triathlons—were because I didn't care what anyone else thought. I had no fear, or care, about other people's opinions of me. I did not overthink the journey I was on. I ignored the opinions of others and "the committee in my head." To master that was peace, the ultimate prize for winning. If I was able to think strategically back in high school, I am sure I would have saved myself from a great deal of unnecessary pain. My "stinkin' thinkin'" would get worse over time as I would become my own biggest liability...

Besides cross-country, I ran track, joined clubs and worked to make this time my own. I had some close, supportive friends. I got my first boyfriend, and guys asked me to school dances. I studied and did well academically.

Along with exercising, I found the easiest way for me to gain a sense of control with my turbulent home life was working. At 15, I got myself a job as a carhop at Sonic. (Yes, a carhop. No, I did not wear roller skates.) The manager knew I was legally not old enough to work, but he hired me. Mom and Dad took me across town to work any shift scheduled. I loved it! I loved the people, and I loved the guests. I even loved picking up the parking lot. (I did not love making onion rings. Holy smell.) I loved that I had money, not a lot, but enough to get a few things I wanted. I thought I "made it" the day I marched into Pegues and bought myself an Izod. That shirt was priceless, and I wore it for every special occasion. Most of the time, I would use money to pay for gas or help Mom.

Towards the end of high school, I got an "editor's pick" job as a sacker at the local Dillon's grocery store on East 4th. Those jobs were hard to come by, and I felt blessed. After a few months packing groceries into paper bags, I moved up to cashier and then hit the big time as a video clerk in "the cage" (now called Customer Service). I believed I had the best job in the world. My responsibilities were renting VHS and Beta movies, as well as the devices that played them, to our guests. Renting out equipment and receiving new movies was the best. I had responsibility and I took it very seriously. I thought I was on the cutting edge of technology, renting movies and players that would be laughed at and outdated in a matter of years. Nonetheless, I felt pretty cool. I loved when a new movie came out because I made sure I rented it for my family first. Oh, the sweet perks of being a Dillon's employee!

Around that time, I bought my first car, a 1982 red Dodge Charger with a gold stripe, from the Babb Twins: Kenny and Kevin. Actually, their dad Ron owned the car, but the twins got a lot of face time in it. Their younger sister Kerri was one of my best friends, and we always harassed the twins for a ride. Getting their old Charger was something else. I am not sure *how* it had an engine in it after the twins drove it.

At Dillon's, I became close friends with two of my high school guy friends who still mean the world to me today—Jeff Keas and Scott Davis. Jeff worked in the cage with me, though he was "big time" over at the cashier window, selling money orders and stamps, processing refunds, and completing other important tasks that took discretionary judgment. Scott worked in the produce section with John, one of my first long-time boyfriends. It was easy for Jeff and me to talk to these two as the cage and produce were right beside each other. The sweet memories of Dillon's on East 4th...

Jeff and I still laugh about the day I got in a wreck on the way to work in my beloved red Dodge Charger. I called the store to let them know what happened, and Jeff answered the phone. The crash was minor. I was on 11th Street, a few miles from work, and a little shaken up. Anyway, the only thing Jeff asked was "Are you going to be late?" Bless his heart. Jeff notes now, as a senior partner with Populous, one of the world's largest and most renowned architecture firms, that his leadership has improved "a little." Seeing as he now designs and oversees the planning of venues for the Olympics and World Cup games, I agree.

I succeeded with a job at Dillon's. The pay and the atmosphere were much better than the carhop...for me and for Mom. I'm not sure how many of my classmates used their paychecks to keep their houses rolling, but for me it didn't seem weird, just a part of daily life. I felt proud to contribute part of my paycheck each month. I was helping Mom and helping Max, even if we fought—and I had saved enough to buy a car. I was scrappy and "got 'er done" before I knew what scrappy looked like. Now they call this innovative. Back then, I never gave up, because quite frankly, I knew giving up was not an option for me or my family.

Though I started to enjoy high school, I never felt like I fit in. I gained confidence because I could see that buried somewhere deep inside me, I was smart and funny. But while I let that side show more, I worried people knew my story at home. I yearned for the day when I could free myself from this feeling of not being enough.

The first taste of being able to develop my own identity, independent of my family history, came my junior year of high school. I attended Sunflower Girl's State at the University of Kansas. Girl's State (and Boy's State) is an incredible learning experience that is still run for high school students across the U.S. Girl's State is a week-long summer leadership and citizenship program sponsored by the American Legion and American Legion Auxiliary for high school juniors. The week away immersed me in learning about our government, elections, debates, and how our political system works. More than anything, I got to be away from home and learn at the same time. It didn't get any better than that.

A handful of friends and I loaded into a bus and headed to KU. There I met the smartest, most hard-working women from all over the state—women who I would later see in college. This was the first place I met my adult self. I blended in, and they did not know my story. I could be me.

Loving and caring. Fun.

A handful of us were elected for state positions and I was one of them. My peers elected me Attorney General for the entire session. It was probably my campaign slogan, which I stayed up all night devising, that did it for me..."Be Bright, Vote Wright!" I wore a flashy light bulb on my head and handed out little light bulb flyers during our campaigns. Or maybe it was just me—girls actually liked me. As part of the position, I got to spend the day with the Attorney General of Kansas, Bob Stephan. What an amazing day. Even more meaningful to me was that the program allowed state officers to invite our parents to the inauguration in Lawrence.

I didn't have enough money for a formal dress for inauguration, but my dear friend Becky Johnson's sister, Monica, let me wear her prom dress. It was strapless and white with lots of frills that went all the way to the floor. An '80s prom dress at its greatest: lots of material with a belt.

The crowd of us girls walked out of our dorms on The Hill at KU that evening in our formal gowns, headed to the ceremony. As I rounded a corner, my dad and stepmom stood there waiting for me. My dad held a bunch of red roses that he brought for me. I was never so proud. He had driven nearly three hours to spend just a few minutes with me. His gesture stirred up in me a feeling I will never forget. He taught me a lesson: The little things really are the big things.

I graduated from high school in May 1986 and headed off to the University of Kansas that fall. College was never an "if" in our house. The question for Max and me was *where* we were going to go to college. I applied to KU, Tulane, and Dartmouth. I am not sure what I thought trying to get into Dartmouth, my dad's alma mater, but I applied. I do not distinctly remember the letters from KU and Tulane, but I do remember how fast the letter from Dartmouth arrived at my house. As quick as I applied, it felt like I received that "thin" letter the next day. Upon opening the "thanks, but no thanks" letter I called my dad. A man of great words, he replied, "You either are not smart enough, or I didn't give enough money." Well said, Dad. Well said.

CHAPTER 4

God's Nos are My Best Yeses

Before I could get to Las Vegas, the casinos, bright lights, limos, private planes, and in every direction the desert before me, I had to make it through college and the incredibly painful time of extreme loss thereafter that took hold of me. I appeared to juggle those years well from the outside, but I was a mess on the inside. I had a God I thought, but I had no concept of who Jesus was. My few and infrequent visits to church as a child only left me with an idea of the love Jesus has for us. I did not understand yet that Jesus can change everything. Without Jesus' guidance, my direction in life came from my will, "brilliance," and the few tools I had in my tool belt. Somewhere in late high school and college, my identity with regards to "whose I was" became hazy.

My home life was okay: Dad was sober, Mom still busting it at work, and Max kept busy with school, sports, and extracurricular activities with his friends. Still, I never felt enough. Not by my dad, and not by my mom. (Though I knew she loved me very much, she worked around the clock.) Not by my friends. No one. I felt I always had to be strong. I took it on myself to help raise Max and keep our family safe. I felt alone in my mind and never belonged, though from the outside, you could never tell (or at least I thought).

I tried using so many unhealthy coping mechanisms to fill my emptiness. Working out. Starving myself, going out with guys and trying alcohol way too early. I started drinking (malt duck: yuck; cherry vodka: worse).

College was good for me. I left Hutchinson and headed to the University of Kansas (some three hours away) in the fall of 1986: the era of Madonna, The Cars, Cameo (don't judge), Lionel Richie, and Bon Jovi. At school, I had the chance to be me. No crazy past to tend with when you leave home…or so I thought. Come to find out if you do not address your past, your hurts and hang ups, it will own you later. Today, I know trauma is real, but back then I thought you tucked that in with everything else in your suitcase and moved on. Unfortunately, not.

I joined Alpha Gamma Delta sorority and made the best of friends. The sorority housed young ladies from all over—small town Kansas, Kansas City, Nebraska, Chicago, Oklahoma. It became home to me. We loved, lived, laughed, and attended KU football and basketball games in Allen Field House…and we studied. (Really!)

We ate at Yellow Sub and Pizza Shuttle, drank beer at The Wheel and The Bull, and found life away from home. These girls have grown into beautiful, amazing women. Teachers, doctors, executives, mommies, and more. I love to see them flourish now that they're in their 40s and 50s. But in those years, they saw and lived with me at my best and worst, and vice versa. Lori, Vicky, Stacia, Maria, Amy, Carla Sue, Gena, and Sara became part of my family away from home. Being the house rush chairman and pledge trainer gave me early experience in leadership and more importantly, taught me to lead with love and boundaries. As much as you adored your girlfriends, they had to wear their dresses, attend their meetings, and make their grades. I loved the responsibility of helping others.

My classes taught me to think and reason. For me it's not so much on the dates of the wars or how to conjugate a word in French. Though all the years of French in high school and college did help me a bit in Paris. OK, not really. I could order a *bouteille de vin* pretty well *avec* some *fromage*. Other than that, all I can do in France is get my family lost.

My college experience was normal, and normal for me was superb. Even at home, things stabilized. Dad's new healthy lifestyle fit him well. My parents came up for Mom's Days and Dad's Days at the house. My father loved KU football games, though the Jayhawks were never fantastic. When he and my brother would come up to visit, we always got to the stadium early to watch the band come out. No football day was too hot or too cold for him. He was one of those men who would watch a football game on TV and listen to another game on the radio (usually the Huskers, if he could).

Then came 1988 at the University of Kansas: the year the Jayhawks won the NCAA basketball championship against Oklahoma. That night, we all cheered for the team who would go down in history as "Danny and the Miracles." After our sorority had a function with a fraternity, we all headed up to campus to celebrate. After I fell on my head (from the shoulders of my guy friends), we headed back to another fraternity to celebrate more. Some of my high school friends drove up from Manhattan (Kansas, not New York) to celebrate with us. KU Basketball is tradition.

Normal for me also included working during college. I babysat, worked at the Watson library, waited tables, and worked at the Sallie Mae Loan Servicing Center. Some jobs beat boredom better than others. Working in the skip tracing department at Sallie Mae made me want to pull my hair out. Who wanted to search for students who defaulted on their loans? No one wanted to hear from me. Library research challenged me. Back then we *manually* researched by using the Dewey decimal system, looking through microfiche, and trolling through The Stacks.

My part-time jobs going back to Sonic and Dillon's gave me more than just gas (and beer) money. They taught me the value of hard work.

 My dad always said, "Be the job great or small, do it well or not at all."

But I always found my goal was to leave my workplace a little better than I found it, or at least make a difference. I also learned early on the value of a caring, involved supervisor. The more the supervisor cared about me and valued my thoughts, the more I cared—even if the job meant sitting in a cube calling students who defaulted on their loans. I also worked during the summers back home for both me and mom to help with bills for her and Max. One summer I waited tables at Donovan's, the hopping restaurant at home during this time. It was like an Applebee's or Ruby Tuesday, without the flair. I absolutely loved to wait tables and then worked as a cocktail waitress in the bar in my khaki shorts and green polo. Don't get any ideas...We are not to Vegas yet. Every night I would come home and spread my tips out on the dining room table. My mom and I would split the cash. I loved helping her.

This is where my scrappy self started trying to be more polished and innovative. I could make future plans and knew what I needed to do to solve problems. I progressed beyond my childhood, when my life was more about "staying in the ring and keep on fighting!"

During college, I lost an important woman in my life. In my freshman year, on October 15, 1986, I got a call from my dad early in the morning. He was quiet, very quiet. He finally got the words out and said my mother's younger sister Aunt Tresa passed away. How can that be? Aunt Tresa was so young.

Aunt Tresa (pronounced Teresa—Mom said they misspelled her name on her birth certificate) was my mother's younger sister, but my dad had called instead of my mom. He was a thoughtful man, as he knew he would be the best to give the news. Dad and Aunt Tresa were buddies. He told me a grain truck at the Nebraska mill where she worked ran her over. A cousin of hers did not see her and backed over her. She died instantly. I sat in my dorm room at GSP Hall, crying and staring at the bulletin board. I convinced myself my dad was wrong. I cried and cried and cried. And begged and begged and begged for this not to be true. I put on my big girl pants and went to class. It was all I knew to do. My Aunt Tresa was the ultra-cool aunt who said what I wanted to say, with words I was not allowed to say. She protected me. She was mentally and physically tough before it was cool for women to be strong. And she drove a truck!

Eventually my mom called, and she was inconsolable. What could I say to my mother who just lost her younger sister? A few days passed, and my family decided they did not want me to miss college to drive to Nebraska. I kept going. I went to class and cried at night. I had been through pain so much in my life that by the time I turned 18, pain felt normal. Still, this was different. I couldn't compartmentalize and turn it off. I couldn't tell my heart to quit hurting.

Graduation came fast. Though I went to college to become a dentist, I came out with a degree in Journalism and Public Relations. My goal going in was to help people smile. Growing up, I would sometimes unbend a paperclip and put on my teeth to have fake braces. To me, braces meant you had money. Actually, my paperclips popped out of mouth and weren't worth all the prestige I never got. It always broke my heart when people half-smiled because of their teeth. My mom always fought this with a fake half-smile.

My dreams of becoming a dentist were shot down, all due to the heinous class organic chemistry. Who came up with that stuff? Who thinks and reasons like that? Not me, obviously. That weed-out class "weeded me out." Dad, who majored in chemistry at Dartmouth, could never understand my "lack of understanding" (I call it failing) when I would call in tears. I dropped the course and decided Journalism and Public Relations sounded fun. Dad shuddered. He was concerned as to how I could pay my bills with a Journalism/PR degree. All I knew was the classes interested me. Some four years after college, I ended up smack in the middle of the casino world, launching my career. Helping others smile would come in a different way.

CHAPTER 5

My Leadership Primer— Housekeeping 101

My first few years after college were not all bad. Not all perfect, but not all bad. I lived in the relative metropolis of Topeka, Kansas, some 30 minutes west of KU. I ended up in Topeka after college because of a boy, a kind guy I met in college who played football at the University of Nebraska.

It all started when I received his fraternity pin at a pinning ceremony in college. A pinning ceremony is a fraternity ritual where a guy gives his fraternity pin to the girl, signifying his commitment to her. The girl announces it (if in a sorority) with a candle-lighting event with her sisters.

One day during my senior year, my sorority sisters and I went downstairs after having some frozen yogurt instead of formal dinner for a candle-lighting announced earlier in the day. I wore a khaki shirt, sweater, and white canvas shoes, not appropriate dress for the occasion and certainly not expecting this event was for me. Our housemother, Camella, and my sorority sisters gathered in a circle and began singing, passing a candle, and reading poems. My closest friends were chosen to read poems, so I *should* have known who was about to get pinned. David, my boyfriend, walked in the AGD living room with long stem red roses and his fraternity pin. I broke down in tears. My girlfriends kept it a surprise, never letting on. I felt alive and loved.

David was originally from Topeka, and I followed him back after I graduated. It wasn't until later on that I would learn why God sent me to Topeka: to meet and befriend David's mother, Jeanne, who would eventually show me the power of a life in Christ.

It took a few months, but I figured out how to live on my own. I moved from waiting tables and hosting at Olive Garden while working odd shifts at a local gym to pay the bills, and on to my first real job: an account executive in an advertising agency.

I was so excited to put on real clothes and go to work, until I understood what being paid "on draw" meant. My boss explained it meant getting advanced on your commission for the month. Whatever I sold in advertising for the month, my commission check would be less the "draw" amount I received at the beginning of the month. And because I never sold any advertising, I actually should have paid back my full salary, but my boss never made me. Thank the Lord! Because my ad sales career wasn't flourishing, I needed to keep working other jobs to keep the electricity on. So, I suited up by day and put the polyester and gym clothes back on for weekends and nights. I was paying all my bills and living on my own. The apartment wasn't luxurious by any means, but it was what I could afford. My mother was horrified the first time she came to Polk Street. It wasn't that I could stand in the living room, kitchen, and bedroom at the same time. Mom was alarmed by the bars on the windows. I told her I had it all under control, but she and I both knew I wasn't living in a safe area. Luckily, I would get to move from that apartment within months.

Then came the second real job. One day when I was on sales calls for the ad agency, I went to the Holiday Inn Holidome on Fairlawn Street in Topeka with my boss. I bopped into the hotel to listen to their needs and learn how we could help them with radio and newspaper advertising. After the meeting, I went back to the office to a phone call from the Holidome. The regional vice president wanted to know if I had any interest in the hospitality business. I told him I knew very little about hotels since my family stayed in drive-up motels when we took our rare trips. He said, "no worries" and told me to come in for a chat.

A couple days later I went back in my Casual Corner navy blue suit, wearing my only blouse, navy shoes, and the uncomfortable L'eggs pantyhose of the day. After my first meeting with the sales team, general manager, and regional vice president, I got a second call. Not about advertising but about a job. The Holidome wanted me to be their front desk manager. I knew nothing about hotels, but this sounded great. They thought my energy was just what the hotel needed. Then they told me about the $18,500 salary.

I screamed. A real salary. I was sold. The job was a mystery, but it sounded fun and meant I'd make enough to quit working nights and weekends at the other jobs. That interview—for a job I hadn't even applied for—marked the beginning of my career in the hotel and casino business.

After about a year at the front desk, I was blessed—yes, blessed—to be "promoted" to executive housekeeper. I knew little about the position beyond cleaning rooms, but my boss told me it was vital to the front desk and hotel. I learned more about myself and others as a leader in this one single position than several of the executive positions I have had. Some of the hardest, most demanding positions in your life will be your biggest gift. Do the job. Do it well. Learn from it.

My office: A storeroom full of toilet paper, Kleenex, sheets, towels, and housekeeping carts tucked away in the back of the second floor. It wasn't what I expected coming out of college, but I was content with it.

My team: The most diligent workers with the biggest hearts. All the housekeepers wanted was to do their job well, get paid, and go home. Work, in some cases, was easier for them than home, which is still the case for workers across the world today. Life is hard. Work is controlled chaos and a safe place for many. Yes, work is *work*, but leaders should help make it a place conducive for employees to a) make a difference, b) be themselves, and c) make a living.

This first job taught me as much as any textbook: how to lead (and with love), how to work hard, and the importance of prioritizing people when building a successful business.

I learned buses don't always arrive on time.

I learned employees get paid on Friday and sometimes don't make it to work on Saturday.

I learned that on Saturdays, I had to clean rooms.

I learned to create a team where people wanted to come to work on Saturdays so they didn't let their teammates down.

I learned how to clean more than one board of rooms in a day.

I learned how to make a mean bed and clean a bathroom till it shone.

I learned that in the world of housekeeping, there is either a fabulous day or a bad day. There is no in-between.

I learned how to laugh when work was hard and reward those who went beyond their job description to help guests and coworkers.

I learned how to make a tasty side dish for the lunches they shared.

I learned that room attendants want their own sections and hate cleaning up after coworkers who ruin their tubs and don't restock their carts.

Most importantly, I learned you can love and lead employees at the same time. This cannot be taught. When employees know you sincerely love them, the tough conversations become easy. From that leadership, employees grow, leaders grow, teams develop, output skyrockets, and it is much easier for companies to make money.

No one had to teach me this at 20 some years of age. Love and leadership come from the heart.

CHAPTER 6

The Plan of the Master Weaver

Our lives are but fine weavings,
That God and we prepare,
Each life becomes a fabric planned
And fashioned in His care.
We may not always see just how
The weavings intertwine,
But we must trust the Master's hand
And follow His design,
For He can view the pattern
From the upper side,
While we must look from underneath
And trust in Him to guide.
Sometimes a strand of sorrow
Is added to His plan,
And though it's difficult for us,
We still must understand
That it's He who fills the shuttle,
It's He who knows what's best,
So we must weave in patience
And leave to Him the rest...
Not till the loom is silent
And the shuttles cease to fly
Shall God unroll the canvas
And explain the reason why—
The dark threads are as needed

In the Weaver's skillful hand
And the threads of gold and silver
In the pattern He has planned."

—Anonymous

I bought this card for a friend after the loss of their family member. I read the card over and over and bought every copy in the store. I revisit this poem every time I lose someone.

"It's He who knows what's best,
So we must weave in patience
And leave to Him the rest..."

There's so much I don't understand. I do not understand why some of the most beautiful, kind people leave this earth too early. But my faith *now* knows 1) God has this, 2) they are in a much better place with their relationship with Christ, and 3) I will see them on the other side.

I lost my beloved Aunt Tresa when I was a freshman in college, and she turned out to be the first of many people close to me who I lost over the next 14 years. After graduating, I lost five more of the most amazing, loving, kind, generous people in my life. There were times that the pain did not stop. A year after finishing college, came another of the unimaginable.

It was December 1991.

I was living in my apartment in Topeka with one of my best friends from middle school and high school. Kerri Babb was the younger sister of the twins I'd bought my first car from. Kerri was always so put together, with her makeup and hair just so. Her big blue eyes, blonde hair, and beautiful cheeks turned heads wherever we went. We went to college together at KU, and Kerri had been my friend since eighth grade. Growing up, Kerri, her best friend Gina Ryder, and I had many a late-night sleepover at the Babb house. We brawled with her twin brothers, Kenny and Kevin, who were two years ahead of us. We were a nuisance to the twins and all we ever wanted, as we got older, was to "borrow" their car.

By 1991, I had settled into my job at the Holiday Inn. Kerri was working a job in Lawrence, and I'd often get home before her. Then came December 11. I got home from work at a decent hour and laid on the couch of our second-floor apartment. I dozed off for a bit and awoke to silence. It was dark and Kerri still wasn't home from work, which was odd because her routine was like clockwork. I waited a bit. I called my mom in Hutchinson and told her I was worried about Kerri. She told me not to worry, "Sometimes people get busy and forget to call. She might just be in traffic." Fine. I waited a little longer and still, no Kerri.

I called her best friend Gina, who lived in Kansas City, and told her I did not know where Kerri was. I was getting really worried. As time passed, my mom, Gina, and I grew desperate, distraught. I was still in my work clothes when I decided to call the highway patrol to tell them my roommate had not returned home from work. I asked if there were any accidents between Topeka and Lawrence. Indeed, there were. The person on the phone said traffic was backed up, and I exhaled, relieved. She was stuck in traffic, I thought. The highway patrol asked what kind of car my roommate drove. I told them a CRX. They thanked me and hung up. I called Mom and Gina a few more times while we all waited. Our apartment phone rang. The person on the line asked if my phone number was "271-5093." I said, "No, my phone number is 271-5092." They thanked me and hung up without an explanation. Strange, but okay. A weird phone call was the least of my worries.

Then came the knock on the door. I opened the door and there stood two troopers, one male and one female. They took off their hats.

I was sure they had everything wrong. They could not be speaking of my roommate. This was not right. I took them into Kerri's room and showed them a picture of her, sure they had the wrong person. They explained that the caller with the "wrong" phone number earlier in the night actually had the "right" phone number. They wanted to make sure someone was at Kerri's residence.

It started getting very foggy.

Kerri was involved in a head-on collision between Lawrence and Topeka. The details are too hard to type; Kerri was the only fatality.

I sat on the couch crying uncontrollably. The phone rang and I went over to the wall to answer it. It was my mom. "Mom, Kerri is…" No, the officers waved at me. No. They told me I could not tell anyone until Kerri's parents were notified. It was too late; I had already let the sentence out to my mom. My mom was grief-stricken. I told her the troopers were at the apartment and I had to go, but she could not say a word to anyone until they called Judy and Ron. I hung up. The phone kept ringing and for the rest of the night I either answered it and lied about Kerri's update or ignored the calls.

The memory of sitting at the dining room table with the troopers still haunts me today. The table was Kerri's—a round wooden Pier One table with wicker chairs. I gave the troopers Kerri's entire life story…told them about her mother and father and her twin older brothers. Lucy, her cat, came out of hiding in the apartment, and that started my sobbing again. We got through the details, and they offered to stay with me until I heard from her parents. Not a chance, I thought, to sit in an apartment with two Kansas State Troopers, feeling like I wanted to get sick because I was to the point of nausea. The troopers said I could call someone to come sit with me. News of the death overwhelmed me as it crystallized into a sickening reality.

I had been dating a new boy, Ray Kempthorne, for a few months and told him what happened. Ray, who would later become my husband, attended Kansas State, about an hour west of Topeka. Ray, who was calm, headed to my apartment.

I convinced the troopers to leave. I told them I was fine, and that I really wanted to be alone with the cat. There I sat. Alone. Kerri was alive as far as I was concerned and had not come home from work yet. I was sure she was going to walk in the door and laugh at me for being so confused. Kerri's beautiful blonde hair, in perfect place, and defined cheek bones would come bouncing in to save the day. But that was not to be. I sat.

Ray finally showed up to comfort me. The phone rang after 10 p.m. It was Ron, Kerri's dad who I had known since eighth grade. I can still hear his voice. Ron said little but let me know he was headed to Topeka from Iowa and would be there in the morning.

I talked to Gina and my mom before I called my dad. He too, said he would drive to Topeka the next morning from Hutchinson. Minutes turned to hours which turned to days. Horrible, horrible days. Her cat Lucy sat at the kitchen table every morning as I ate my cereal and cried. She didn't even like me. Kerri's mom and dad had a funeral in our hometown at First Presbyterian. The service was beautiful, just like Kerri. I remember staring at the red roses decorating the church during the service as they played "O Holy Night" and "Friends are Friends Forever" by Michael W. Smith. I was filled with sadness and grief.

Nothing mattered anymore. How does a God I trust let this happen? My God would never allow it. Kerri was 23 years young and an incredible, exceedingly kind person. She was funny, beautiful, bright, witty, and made this world a better place. People loved to be around her. Why would God take her?

"It's He who knows what's best,
So we must weave in patience
And leave to Him the rest..."

Every time I went back to Hutch, I always took fresh roses to her graveside. I spent many days sitting and talking with her. Our childhood neighbor, Judy, took flowers out to the grave every year on Memorial Day. I am not sure if her family knew who brought those flowers, but Kerri did.

I am still in touch with her family—her mother Judy and her stepfather Steve; her father Ron and his wife Jeri; and the twins. A hug from any of them has a little of Kerri in it.

My heart still hurts for them, and at times I don't know how to speak with them about the loss. I do know they like for me to share my stories of Kerri. Sometimes when I hear a song on the radio that reminds me of her, I take a picture of the radio and send it to them on Facebook Messenger.

They are my family. They always will be.

I still think of Kerri often. When I run, I talk to her and the many others I have lost. Sometimes I cry (mostly when I hear "The Dance" by Garth Brooks), but usually thinking of Kerri and others inspires me to do my best remembering; tomorrow is never promised.

Christmas came and went in Topeka.

By 1993, I transferred from my first hotel job to a new Holiday Inn in a Kansas City suburb, Lenexa. I was sad to leave my friends at the Holidome in Topeka, but it was time to move. I was also ecstatic to be moving out of operations (front desk and housekeeping) and into sales. Later on, I learned

I would rather "clean it, dish it, or check it in" than sell it. It would take a few years to learn I was not a salesperson.

I started to get serious with my boyfriend Ray, who I had met at the wedding of my high school friend from Dillons, Scott Davis, and sorority sister, Lori Holzapfel. Ray and I were engaged within a year of meeting. My life became filled with the festivities of wedding planning, but stuffed deep down inside was the sadness of losing Kerri. It helped my mind handle the grief I felt over the loss of my friend.

In November 1993 at Countryside United Methodist in Topeka, Ray and I married. Our whole family was there except those of Ray's family who lived in the Netherlands. We brought in an old trolley, and the ceremony was held at a quaint church. Our wedding was perfect in every way, and we celebrated surrounded by both our parents, our brothers, our family, and friends. Little did we know our wedding night would be the last time both sets of parents and all our family would be together. When we left for our honeymoon Saturday night, November 20, it was the last time Ray ever saw his mother alive.

Upon returning from our honeymoon cruise, I went back to work at the Holiday Inn. I had moved to Kansas City the summer before, as Ray and I decided to live there once married. He was already in town living with my high school buddy Jeff Keas.

Less than two weeks after the wedding, the phone rang at my desk at the hotel. I could barely understand Ray over the phone. It was his mother, Miep; she was dead. Along with two other women, she had been killed by a semi in an automobile accident outside his hometown of Spring Green, Wisconsin. "No. No. What? No." God, where are you? Again? A friend of his at Southwestern Bell Yellow Pages brought Ray from his office to our apartment. We threw a few things in the car and headed for Wisconsin. My heart hurt so bad for Ray. He kept saying, "Oh Miep. My Miep," as he cried tears of pain. There were no words.

His mother, Miep VanEverdingen, was one of the classiest, kindest, most positive, beautiful women to walk this Earth. She had a sweet, perfect Dutch accent. Born in the Netherlands in 1931, she came to Washington D.C. in 1962 and worked with a Dutch diplomat as a nanny. She worked as a nurse at The Doctor's Hospital in D.C. and met Ray's dad Gerald, a physician, on a blind date. They married soon after. Though Miep did not return to the Netherlands to live, she was extremely close to her family, talking to them often and making trips home.

Ray has a beautiful family, and it was a very hard time for him, his father, and his younger brother Guy. We waited for her Dutch family to arrive from the Netherlands, including her 91-year-old mother, Oma. Oma was somehow both feeble and strong. Ray and his family had a celebration of life for Miep that was beautiful, stoic, and perfectly set at St. John's Catholic Church in Spring Green. For months, my new husband could not be consoled; some days were better than others. My heart hurt for him. We went months without opening wedding presents or looking at wedding pictures; I moved the gifts to the spare bedroom, so we didn't have to stare at them in the living room. As seasons passed, we found that opening the presents and looking at the pictures was what we needed to heal, but only when Ray was ready.

And then in the next two years, I would lose two cousins far too young - the son and son-in-law of my mother's oldest sister Darlene.

After Tresa died, it felt impossible that my two cousins would be gone too. In June 1994 my cousin Carol's husband, Jim Bachman, passed away at 39 from a brain tumor. He was an incredibly lovely man, a great businessman and photographer.

He and my cousin Carol had four little boys at the time—Philip, Brian, Neil and Todd. My last memory of Jim was at our wedding. The day after the wedding, Jim helped my dad load up the piles of wedding presents. I always saw Jim's love for others in his humor, his sensitivity, and through the lens of his camera, where he never missed a memory.

Two years later my cousin, John Luce (Carol's younger brother) died at 37 from an infection in his heart valve that caused a blot clot. John left his wife (also named Carol) with two little boys, Aaron and Logan. To make the situation harder, John's wife received a call later that night and learned that her mother, Martha, had an aneurysm and was going to die. The twin tragedy was unfathomable, out of nowhere. Within those two years, six little boys in the same family lost their fathers. Carol Bachman and Carol Luce persevered for those six little boys, and still do to this day.

It piled up: first Tresa, then Kerri, Miep, Jim, and John. I wasn't good at handling my pain, and the pain of their immediate families piled up on me too. I was an empath—experiencing others' pain—before I knew what an empath was. To be able to help was a gift and a curse.

Loss became a norm in my life. I never thought of myself as a victim but more mourned for those who lost. I was deeply sad for a while and cried at random times. Most people never knew about any of my past losses because I worked to hide that part of my life. I decided I was not going to let it define me, or at least that was my goal. I wanted to be happy, and I wanted for others to be happy, too.

Loving others was becoming complex. I wanted to love, but from a distance. That way, I couldn't be hurt if people left. Along the way, I found happiness in helping others find happiness, but I know today it was only a temporary fix. I could only stuff it inside for so long before I would crash and burn.

My brother and I still talk about living with loss and hurt. We did not know any different. Max had loss on top of the deaths in our family: suicides of friends in high school and college. He and I were up for a battle we didn't know was in front of us.

Looking back, I believe I know why God led me to Topeka. Not for pain. Not for a boy. I believe God brought me to Topeka to befriend Jeanne, my college boyfriend's mother. Jeanne Trupp was a God-fearing, Jesus-loving woman and through her I was introduced to God and Jesus Christ.

Jeanne worked at Countryside United Methodist Church. I had met her on more than one occasion during college as David was very close to his family, and it seemed his mother was always at church. He had three older siblings who were as lovely as David.

This was a family I wanted to emulate. There was so much love and so much God, that even trying times seemed okay.

Back in those first months in Topeka, when I wasn't working, applying for jobs, or spending time with David, I was with his family. I attended services with them and went to church events. I felt so at peace, like when I was a little girl again at the First Christian Church back home. I stepped up to teach Sunday School for the two- and three-year-olds. It was important for me to teach that age because I was 100% sure I could answer their questions about God and Jesus. Any older and I would have been making a list of their questions to bring home and research each week. It was more of a babysitting job than teaching, but I loved it. I knew now I wanted Jesus to be the Lord and Savior of my life. At Countryside United Methodist Church in Topeka, I gave myself to Christ. Pastor David Mitchell baptized me, and I knew I was free from all my pain and suffering; I was enough. While I knew this in my head, I did not wholeheartedly feel it in my heart yet.

CHAPTER 7

The Casino Life—And Flying Elvi!

I f someone had told me as a girl I would grow up to run casinos, I would
have told them they were crazy. I knew nothing about casinos. I had never
been to Las Vegas, Lake Tahoe, or Atlantic City, and movies like *The Hangover*
and *Ocean's Eleven* were years away. The closest I got to gambling was playing
bingo with my mother. From commercials, I knew casinos had slot machines,
table games with well-dressed executives, beautiful showgirls, and entertainment with the best stars. To me, the casino business was a world of mystery.

But by 1994 in North Kansas City, Missouri, everything changed.

I had been working at the Holiday Inn outside Kansas City for about three
years, when a coworker went to work for the new casino in town: Harrah's
North Kansas City.

I heard the casino was being built "North of the River" and was a dirt
lot and a shell of a building. A beautiful, grand brick structure standing tall
with a clock tower outlined in neon, but still a shell. As it turned out, this
beauty of a building wasn't the casino but the restaurants, retail, and back-of
house areas that support the gambling side. The "casino" part of this operation hadn't arrived yet. Arrived, you say? Yes, at that time in the Midwest,
the casinos were merely riverboats. Land-based casinos were then limited
nationally, but a few state governments legalized gaming to help increase
their tax base: Illinois, Indiana, Iowa, and Missouri.

Within a few weeks of my coworker leaving the Holiday Inn for Harrah's,
she called to see if I had any interest in a manager position with the casino.
I was skeptical, but I let her explain the position: guest services manager.
Sounded cool, even if I was currently a director at the hotel. The manager
would be responsible for ticketing (in the early days we sold tickets to get into

48

the casino, and customers paid to gamble), wardrobe, valet, and PBX (the phone center). That sounded pretty good. I knew I could handle it. I sent her my resume to pass on.

I received a phone call from Harrah's North Kansas City, and they asked me to fill out an application and interview. The casino offices were offsite in downtown North Kansas City, a quaint suburb of Kansas City.

Downtown North Kansas City was only a few blocks long, had brick buildings, beautiful trees, and a little restaurant the new casino executives would invade as more and more leaders came on board.

The biggest problem for me was I didn't know how to get "North of the River." For people from the Kansas City area, this directional term "North of the River" is used by those people who live on the Kansas side of Kansas City to get you to the Missouri side. Traveling to Missouri was like driving to Egypt because I hadn't lived in the area for long. Nonetheless, I got specific directions from my coworker, put on my best suit, and headed north.

At that interview, I met the one woman who would single-handedly make the biggest impact on my life besides my mother.

Joann Hauser makes this world a better place. Upon meeting her in the temporary offices in downtown North Kansas City, I could tell this woman was "crisp." A polished, thin lady in a business suit perfect for New York, her red, shoulder-length hair was like the fire that burned inside of her. She was stunning in every way, from her perfectly manicured nails down to her polished shoes. Joann was as bright as she was beautiful, and more gorgeous inside. If you look up the qualities of a talented leader in any leadership book, it has Joann Hauser's name written all over it. She had high standards *and* was compassionate. She was a teacher, but also a learner.

People loved to work for Joann because she made us into better people. She pushed us to be our best—personally and professionally. I also never knew how she could remember the financials to all her departments to the penny. Her business acumen was as on target as her precision in every action. What a true blessing God would tee up in my life as an eventual mentor and best friend, through the good and the bad.

But my initial thought the day I met Joann was, "There is no way I am going to get this job from this lady."

Joann and I talked for more than two hours, but I could have sat with her for hours more. I came back for a second interview with other executives, and they were as affecting as Joann.

Within a couple weeks I had the job. I was going to work in a casino, and I still hadn't seen the inside of one. As Paul Martinelli (president of the John Maxwell Team) says, "Do it scared!" And that is what I did.

As many people who move into in a new industry can attest, the beginning was humbling. The lingo was mind-boggling. In a casino, the jargon is endless. There was the *pencil*: a scheduling area for tables and slots; *jockeys*: valet attendants; the *cage*: the casino cashier where the money is located; *theoretical*: the expected worth of the casino guest. Add in the riverboat aspect of this location, and there is the *head*: the ship's toilet, the *hold* below the deck, *deckhands*...and the list goes on.

With time, I got the hang of our goals as a leadership team. In a little over 90 days, we had to be ready to open a first-class gaming experience. It was daunting to think about what we had to accomplish before opening to ready the casino and restaurants to wow our guests. I knew one thing for sure: I was glad I was not one of the gaming leaders. On top of scheduling, hiring, training, wardrobe, construction, and inventory, this team of leaders had to hire and train employees to fix slot machines and deal cards in a market where gaming did not exist. How could they hire people for skills that were not prevalent in the area? This is when I learned you "hire for fit; train for skill." For the table and slot managers and directors, it was old hat. For me, knee-deep in my own staffing, training, IT requirements, and the works, I could not imagine adding that to the mix.

Hours of planning became days, and days became weeks. The days were long and challenging, but the work was exhilarating, and I was learning.

A casino is a well-oiled machine. Table games. Slots. Security. Surveillance. Wardrobe. Cage and money movement. Restaurants. Human Resources. Facilities. Environmental Services. PBX. Valet. All those departments, and many more, work together to give guests the luxurious casino experience they expect; however, all departments are not equal, and there is a strong pecking order I'd get to understand well during my time at this first casino job.

Casino comes first. Every other department comes second. The casino made the money and all 50+ other departments supported the revenue stream.

Though slot machines make casinos more money, everyone treated the dealers with a sort of reverence, and other employees shied away from their lunch tables in the employee dining room. They were the "Big Men and Women on Campus." There is a certain panache to being a dealer. They wore crisp uniforms and stood watch over their tables. As far as wages were concerned, they made the most of any employees between their base pay and tokes (tips). Over time, gaming companies and leaders included other non-gaming amenities such as food and beverage, retail, and spa into understanding the value of guests and their spending. But the casino was the heart of the operation.

I *vividly* remember the day I was indoctrinated into the casino-first mentality. Harrah's added a hotel tower, and I was promoted to hotel manager. I was called into a meeting to discuss strategies for setting rates and planning room blocks. Having spent the last few years in the hotel world, I was well accustomed to this sort of hotel yield meeting. On this particular day, I represented the entire hotel leadership team and met with several members of the casino (table games and slots) leadership team. I tell you, if you have never worked with people from Atlantic City, they will bring you up to speed real quick to their way of life, and it starts with "I don't mean any disrespect" or "not for nothing." We were discussing what our hotel pricing strategy would be based on occupancy, groups, and events, and everything came to a halt. Each member of the casino team took turns telling me whose hotel it was, and it was not mine. The rooms belonged to the casino, and the casino leadership was going to decide rates, not me. I refused to back down. I came back at them with my thought on basing the rates on occupancy and demand. Then they solidly shut me down with casino math. "Casino guests go in hotel rooms. Everyone else gets a room after that." I pushed my chair away from the conference table and listened. I held back the tears and fought the urge to go screaming out of the conference room.

But as I listened, I realized these guys were right. I had never heard about yielding a hotel the casino way, meaning casino leadership would determine what rooms they needed and when. It wasn't just the message, but also how it was delivered: straightforward and in my grill, from a room full of peeps from Atlantic City. It was very clear, very quickly. Patrick Browne, who was the director of slots at the time, jumped in and told the casino guys to back down. Thank the Lord for that man. The meeting concluded, and I walked out with them. The funny thing was the gaming guys were cool, like it never happened, like that was how business always went down. The next day, I got an apology from many of the people who had been in that room—most of whom are my friends to this day. They baptized me into the casino world, and I learned. The learning hasn't stopped for more than 24 years.

I share this story because you can and should move into a new industry. Some of the best leaders I worked with in the casino business were from other worlds: hotels, credit card organizations, and high-end restaurants. The diversity of thought was second to none. Diverse employee backgrounds are important both for the company and for the careers of their employees.

My time at Harrah's North Kansas City in the early '90s was amazing. I had never worked that hard in my entire life. Opening a casino meant 12- to 16-hour days minimum, seven days a week for months, but I didn't mind. Learning how to staff, create training, develop uniforms, install technology, and build a business exhilarated me. While I didn't know it at the time, this team would be one of the best teams I worked with in my entire casino career. Communication was top-notch. Being able to communicate effectively is a critical attribute which is incredibly difficult to develop and maintain across any organization. The challenges to clear communication only increase within a large, complex startup. The communication worked because it was led at the top by Jay Sevigny, our general manager. Jay was brilliant, calm, and predictable. His poise kept everyone at ease and his communication kept the ever-growing team aligned. Jay would grow to become President and COO of various casino, resort, and gaming supplier companies before he retired. What a blessing it would be for me to see and be led by the best right out of the gate.

In casinos, your ability to use communication and teamwork skills to respond to a crisis was constantly being tested. The more leaders work on developing those skills, the better employees will be at responding to problems when they pop up. Case in point: "The Flying Elvi!"

In every casino story there has to be an "Elvis" story, or at least a sighting. My story is no exception—this so-called crisis put our team's skills to the test.

When I was the guest services manager in North Kansas City, someone much higher than me decided to ask the Flying Elvi to come visit our casino. A group of Elvis impersonators was going to jump out of a plane and parachute onto our property. They were extremely popular in Vegas at the time, but being in the Midwest, this was something new and novel to our region. Since they had never visited Missouri before, it was hard to predict how many people would want to come out to see the Flying Elvi jump.

Casinos regularly sent out offers for everything from events and hotel stays, to giveaways and concerts based upon many marketing factors. The goal was to get a response that was just right...or as close to right as possible.

Harrah's North Kansas City definitely did not get the response right that day. Let me put it this way: Harrah's backed up interstates and highways all over Kansas City as carloads of people drove up to our casino to get in and watch the jump.

And where was I?

Outside with Patrick Browne, then leader of Slot Operations and now a casino CEO, directing traffic in complete chaos. Cars came from every direction, and we had no place to park them. I stood outside for hours while guests screamed at me. My goal was to prevent an accident. The Flying Elvi jumped, and our guests finally left.

That day, I learned working at a casino meant wearing professional, comfortable, seasonal work attire and *always* bringing tennis shoes and a backup outfit in case things got crazy. It took me days to be able to walk again with all my blisters, but I learned. Baptism by jumping Elvis impersonators sticks with you!

That was not the last casino event where our redemption rate was much higher than our predicted guest response. Like when airlines overbook a flight, casino promotions sometimes exceed our anticipated response rate, creating a shortage of gifts like t-shirts, blenders, pots, and pans for our guests. Bless it. More guests have yelled at me because we ran out of blenders than for any other reason. At times like this, I had to smile. I also learned I would not allow our guests to yell or berate our employees. I will easily jump ahead of an employee to take yelling and finger-pointing for service breakdowns that rarely deserved a screaming session. Leaders owe it to their employees to stand in the way and sometimes fire a guest.

The chaos of those first few years eventually settled down, and I found normalcy in North Kansas City. Our first hotel tower opened successfully under Joann's watchful eye. With her background in hotels at Embassy Suites, she didn't miss a detail, from the look, to the operation, to the yield of the hotel. Because of my Holiday Inn experience, I ran the front desk, the bell stand, and reservations, and I thrived under Joann's tutelage. God truly blessed me by allowing me to be trained by the best. Many in the casino world today can still say, "Joann Hauser made me better!"

Then one day, Joann decided it was time for her to retire. Many of us, myself included, let out a heavy sigh. My mentor was leaving. On the bright side, the general manager allowed me to temporarily oversee all the rest of her departments until her successor was named. That meant I was in charge of operations, security, facilities, and environmental services, to name a few. Other directors called me the "Director of Everything Else." Though I didn't get a promotion, I loved learning, growing, and working harder. I was just fine without the money because I knew it would all come in time. And it did. After nearly five years in the casino business, I was promoted to the Director of Services. Both honored and proud, I was not going to let my team down.

My years working at Harrah's were also some of the most fun years of my career. The stress of the job was high, and I felt the responsibility of the work I was doing, but the way the team got through was by sharing our absurd stories of experiences with guests and employees. The best stories were much like those on America's Funniest Home Videos. Casinos have surveillance everywhere, so if there weren't enough people around to witness the 30 second spot, you could always replay it for your friends. This story will forever be ingrained in my brain.

On most Saturday nights, casino executives regrouped in the night to chat and shared how the evening was going—-usually over a cup of coffee. At one such break, our Food and Beverage Director shared a guest complaint that even he did not know how to answer.

That night, a guest in the buffet got the attention of the director through one of the employees at the restaurant. When the director got to the lady's table, she told him her soup was very, very salty. Salty, he thought? That sounds odd given the soups he was offering that night. He went on to ask the lady which soup she had eaten. She pointed to a bowl beside a tray of crab legs. "There!" she pointed. And with that, he knew which soup she had eaten— almost an entire bowl of melted, salted butter. She ladled up the butter for the crab legs and ate it like soup. Our director was almost without words.

He told her what she ate, and offered his apology for her night ahead. She knew, without him saying, it was going to be a long, long night and our casino had nothing to do with the "saltiness" of it.

And then there was this story...

One cool, sunny morning, I was out on the casino floor when I got a call from a valet supervisor to come down to valet. I asked the young man on the other end, who sounded nervous, to let me know what was going on, so I had an idea before I showed up. All he said was, "You may want to talk to Ryan." We will call him Ryan for the sake of this conversation, but he knows who he is. I liked this jockey a lot.

Ryan said it would be best if I came down. I got to the valet desk, and he walked me to the parking garage. There it was. A truck with a "funny car" bed open. Wide open with the hydraulics showing. (Imagine a dump truck with its back bed open to dump sand—that is what this truck looked like!) Ryan proceeded to tell me the driver (one of our regulars) told him he could try the funny car and push a certain button to see the back truck bed tilt open at an angle. So, what does any young man do when he's given permission to try out a funny car? He tries it! 😊

"Ryan, what were you thinking? Just because a guest tells you can try his car out, does NOT mean you can try his car out." He said he understood, but it was way too late. I got the valet ticket and got a hold of security. They looked at me and their eyes said, "Bless your heart, Dawn." We called around and got ahold of the guest, and amazingly enough he was so kind and calm. I told him we would pay to have it fixed.

Ryan looked at me and asked, "Now what?" That was one of the days— and there were more than a few—when I had to tell my employee to fill out an accident report, get drug tested, and I would be in touch. The guest was fine; we ended it on great terms, and the repair cost was minimal. Ryan ended up staying with us and being one of the best valet attendants we had. He worked any day asked, any shift and always ran to get guests' cars (which was a bigger deal than you think). The guests loved him. After that day, Ryan knew he was one write-up away from losing a job many young guys would like to have. He made good money, and the thought of losing it inspired him. I would like to have more Ryans in my lifetime.

The biggest blessing in the casino industry—in addition to the amazing medical benefits, 401Ks, vacation time, and college reimbursement—was the training HR provided, especially working for Harrah's Entertainment.

Harrah's designed, created, and offered training to everyone at every level. We were trained not only on how to do a specific job, but how people ought to be treated, and how to handle upset guests. Employees and leaders were taught how to create and maintain a healthy company culture, which was the key to a company's success. In the casino business, we all had similar slot machines, table games, restaurants, events, promotions…The casino must continually update and refresh these offerings to stay relevant for their market, but the real differentiator was the employees. How well employees do can be predicted by company culture.

So goes the culture, so goes the business.

Happy employees = Happy guests = Happier financials. That became the heartbeat of Harrah's Entertainment. The training wasn't limited to when we were first hired. It never stopped, and it was always fresh. As employees grew in their position, so grew their training. Harrah's started to bring together executives annually to learn from, train with, and hear from best-in-class leaders from around the world including Colin Powell, Pat Summitt, Rick Patino, and Benjamin Zander, the conductor of the Boston Philharmonic.

The casino wasn't going through the motions; their investment in my coworkers and me was genuine. We knew our senior-most leaders cared about us by the way they talked to us and by how quickly bullies or ineffective leaders were ushered out the door. At Harrah's, there was accountability for everyone.

Now that I was one of the leaders, I didn't want to let my team down. My team was every employee in each of the departments I supervised and grew to include everyone in the company. I considered myself responsible for employees anywhere and at every level.

God also gave me people in this industry that changed my perspective of the world and my life. This was not limited to the people I worked for, but also included those I managed and supervised myself. Case in point: Majok Tong. Majok Tong came to work for Harrah's North Kansas City in 1995. Majok was hired in environmental services, the team tasked with cleaning the casino, along with a few of his friends: Anthony, Tong, Dien, and others. Their English was poor at best, but even though it was difficult to communicate, the big smiles on their faces were enough to capture your heart. One would never know that behind Majok's smile was a tragic story. His story, which he shared with me, changed me forever.

Majok lived in South Sudan in the Dinka tribe. In 1993, Majok was wounded in the Sudanese Civil War; he was shot nine times and both of his arms were broken. He knew he had to get out of his country or die, like his mother and father, who fought in the army against the Northern Sudanese. After the shootings and with two broken arms, Majok was taken by a medical team to Kenya, where he stayed for eight months to get well. After those eight months under medical care, he was moved to a refugee camp. There he struggled in horrible conditions with extreme heat and little food or water. At that point, Majok was losing hope. He never gave up because he was with his younger brother and two cousins, and they helped each other mentally and physically. He wanted to be there for them. The foursome was eventually sent to another refugee camp in Kenya, near the Somali border. It was there that his group was informed that the United Nations was going to help them get to the United States. Majok, his brother, and two cousins then traveled to Nairobi, the capital of Kenya, for a medical review and check-up. After all four passed the health exams, they heard they were headed to the U.S. In 1995, the mighty team traveled to Kansas City, Missouri, and their lives would be changed forever, especially thanks to the assistance of the Don Bosco Center, a Kansas City community center.

Soon Majok and some of his Sudanese friends made it to Harrah's North Kansas City. In 2000, Majok became a U.S. Citizen and in 2001, he married his wife, Adet, also from Southern Sudan.

By the time he showed up at Harrah's, Majok still wore the scars of his life in Sudan. One was visible on the back of his arm, where a bullet had hit him. His forehead was striped with the traditional markings of manhood in the Dinka tribe. As Majok's English got better, he shared his entire story with me. I fought back tears during our talks together. When he returned to the memories of his time in Sudan, I could see hurt cloud his eyes. Then he would smile one of the most beautiful smiles I have ever seen, and the pain would all go away for me, and only for the moment. I cannot imagine the memories of his family and country that Majok must have carried in his daily thoughts.

Over the holidays, my husband and I visited his apartment and brought over meals for him and his friends. I always liked going to his apartment. It was in an area that was not so safe near downtown Kansas City—old and run down. My husband and I went during the day and we never felt unsafe, though I am sure we stood out. The apartment was sparsely furnished with a couch and a table. Even with the starkness of the living area, there was a peace about the apartment with all the pictures of their Sudanese family and friends. We laughed because I could not see his photos well; most of them were located near the ceiling at his sight line. Majok and his friends shared the stories behind each picture.

Over time our friendship grew. Majok loved telling me stories about Manute Bol, also from the Dinka tribe, who came to the U.S. to play in the NBA. Ray and I would take Majok and his friends to the Kansas City Zoo, and they had fun at the Africa exhibit. They laughed, pointed, and spoke Dinka most of the time. I hold a photo of one of our zoo trips close to my heart. There are 10 of us in the picture including Majok, looking sharp in a suit. He had dressed for the outing and I loved him more for it. Thinking of this time with Majok makes me smile to this day and get a bit teary-eyed.

People like Majok have filtered into my life. I know God put them in my path for a reason. When I was standing up for the right thing, I had people like Majok in my mind and in my heart. After learning what he and his friends went through to get from Sudan to Kansas City, I owed it to them to develop a work environment where they could use their God-given talent to succeed and be their best, especially since they'd been through so much to get to Harrah's. Majok gave me perspective like no one else ever had. My trials and tribulations pale in comparison to the genocide he endured, and yet he could come to work every day at Harrah's with a smile.

Everyone has a story. For decades, I have heard that coming to work is emotionally easier than being at home for many people. For this reason, leaders should not take their job lightly. Providing a healthy company culture and a safe work environment where employees can prosper is not only the right thing to do for business, but the right thing to do, period.

Majok worked for Harrah's North Kansas City for 25 years in environmental services, security, and table games. Today, he and Adet have six children, five boys and one girl.

A couple years ago I tried reaching out to Majok because I kept seeing photos of him on the casino Facebook page. I contacted a couple friends who still work at the casino and each told me that no one named Majok worked there. But I kept seeing his sweet face and smile on Facebook. Then one day, I found his profile on Facebook, tagged in a photo. Majok was *actually* named Pawil. It was such a happy day!

Then, I remembered when he and his friends first came to the casino, they had explained that what we were calling them were not their real names. When the immigration officer asked what their names were, they smiled, nodded their heads, and agreed. On one of our many talks together, Majok and his friends had told me their real names, hoping one day to have them back in America. But at the time, they said it was the least of their worries. Pawil and I have since exchanged phone numbers and texts. Then would come the day I would hear his kind, Dinka voice. It was a day of laughter and tears. He recounted his story for me in South Sudan, his trek to America and his new family. His voice had not changed. His English, however, was incredible. I cried as I thanked him for changing my life. He asked me to promise if I came to Kansas City to find him. Pawil, that is a promise.

Friendships like this one reminded me what my true purpose was while I worked at the casino, or frankly anywhere: to make a difference in the workplace; to make a difference in people's lives; to help with abuse from a spouse or partner; to help in addiction. I focused on one person at a time, one day at a time. I wanted to be the person they could trust, believe in, and come to for advice, to be someone who I did not always have. Work was a place for many (myself included) that was much more comfortable than home. The longer I worked, the more I learned that I received way more from each of these amazing people than they could ever gain from me.

CHAPTER 8

My Dad's 8-Pound Gift

After a few years, Ray and I decided to try to have a baby. Unfortunately, we found this didn't seem to be in the cards for us. I was unable to get and stay pregnant. Over the course of a few years, I had two miscarriages and an ectopic pregnancy. It was eight years before I would successfully carry a child to term.

So, we lived and worked, and life was agreeable. My mom and brother kept on. Mom was working, working, working, and Max was enjoying college at Kansas. Dad was doing well, really well, for some time. He was still working at Cessna, which became Eaton. He went back to school to get his master's degree and was head-over-heels in love with his wife, Dee. Max and I could tell. We gained a stepbrother, a stepsister, and a dog Dad really loved. "Jo-Jo the Wonderdog" was what he called his ferocious Shih Tzu. He loved that dog as much as he loved his family. Jo-Jo the Wonderdog followed him *everywhere*.

Sadly, Dad got divorced. He loved Dee, and I know she loved him, but it was over. I am not really sure of the reasons, but it wasn't for me to know. My dad's heart broke. Then things started to go south for him.

The first warning sign came in the late '90s. I can't remember the exact date, though I know I was working at Harrah's North Kansas City when the call came from Dad's administrative assistant. She said she thought Dad was drinking.

Oh, Lord.

Ray and I packed up and headed to Hutchinson. My dad was a mess. We couldn't understand why he relapsed after 12 years of sobriety; we knew he needed help. We sat with him, listened to his craziness and figured out where to take him for treatment, which was no easy feat with his insurance. Ray and I decided to take him to Wichita, which was about an hour away, with no map and no real knowledge of how to get to the hospital. So off we headed in the general direction. It was my drunk dad who called out directions in between his rantings and ramblings. I don't know how he knew where to turn, but he did. We let him drink and smoke his cigarettes in the front seat. I rolled down his window and grew lost in my own thoughts. He had been doing so well. How did this happen? I was in so much pain again. It was like when I was little, feeling guilty and out of control.

We got him to the hospital and left him. A few days later, my brother Max and I could talk to him. He was so quiet again and somber. It would be a long time till he got out. He thanked me in a letter I've since laminated.

Dad hurt for himself and for us. Max and I hurt for him, asking each other how 12 years of sobriety went away so fast. I now know all who fight with sobriety have only the day in front of them. Whether you have 12 minutes, 12 hours, 12 days, months, or years. After he got out of the hospital, Dad sat me down and explained to me he thought he "had it," that he could drink just one drink and beat alcoholism. He thought maybe everyone was wrong, and he wasn't an alcoholic. It makes me sad to think of him talking about his pain.

Dad went back to AA and work at Eaton. He worked up until the day he retired from Eaton. I remember his sweet retirement party where employees from every department and level at the plant came to join his celebration. My dad had a beautiful heart for his coworkers.

But three years later, I was shown again the fragility of his sobriety. Dad had been MIA for a few weeks. I had tried calling his home phone more times than I could count with no answer. I called Mom and asked her to drive by his house. He wouldn't answer the door. Mom helped me find him in an old hotel. Dad relapsed a second time. My Dartmouth-grad, brilliant, hilarious, kind father was holed up, hiding in a hotel room. I was in so much pain.

This time, my brother and I drove to Hutchinson. Though we had a lot to talk about, we spoke few words on that three-hour drive home. Max and I sat at Dad's house—he had left the hotel at this point, caught—and I was struck by how similar this visit was to the one I'd made with Ray three years prior. This time, it was worse because Dad held nothing back. Max and I sat there on the couch and silently took in his slurred excuses and piercing, yelled words. He was completely reckless, drinking straight vodka and smoking in the living room of his small apartment. We finally got him in the car and headed back to Wichita for treatment. I knew my dad's health could not keep this up. When we arrived at the hospital, his oxygen level was near 50 percent.

Watching your parent die is horrific—be it suddenly or with an extended illness. There is no easy way to watch them pass, only pain. My coping mechanisms were pretty on point, or, so I thought. Buckle up, take care of family, and pour myself more into work. Hindsight being 20/20, had I had a relationship with Christ at this time, my life would be very different.

All I wanted to do was help keep my dad sober, and I was watching him die before my eyes. Why couldn't I help keep him sober? Didn't he love me and Max? This went through my mind daily for a decade.

Dad and I talked frequently after that, usually after church every Sunday. But one day in June 2000, he didn't pick up for our weekly call. My stomach knotted at the silence on the other end of the line. It felt wrong.

I called the local police in Hutchinson and asked if they would go by my dad's new duplex and do a welfare check. I waited. An hour later, having heard nothing, I called the police again. The dispatcher who answered the phone said I needed to "talk to someone else." I knew what those words meant. Another person got on the phone and told me my dad was deceased. The 911 dispatcher said they had been waiting for law enforcement and a chaplain in Lenexa to pass the news on to me.

The air left my lungs.

How could my dad be dead? Was he alone? What had happened? I was no longer aware of what I was saying to the dispatcher. I knew I had to call my brother who lived a few minutes away. An old fraternity brother of Max's answered my call. I told him I was on the way over because our dad had died. His friend passed the phone over to Max immediately, and I ended up telling him on the phone. Within a couple hours, Max, Ray, and I headed home to Hutchinson, afraid of what was ahead of us. I listened to Sting's songs "Desert Rose" and "Brand New Day" over and over on my CD player in the car. I bawled. Max held it together better than me, but not by much.

We soon found out Dad had probably been dead since Thursday, about four days before. The hardest part to think about was that he had died alone. It breaks my heart to this day. His fearless companion, Jo-Jo the Wonderdog, was licking his face when they found him.

Then I found out he drank himself to death.

Our friend, a police officer, had done the welfare check. They cleared away his bottles before we came over, but it was obvious the alcohol killed him. How does this happen? And to my dad? He was brilliant. He knew better. But his disease did not care one bit.

On top of my grief, I felt guilty because I did not save him from himself. No matter how hard I tried to save him, my dad was dead.

We got to Hutchinson and stayed with Mom. She, too, was upset. Though they were no longer together, they were friends. She lost him, and all the tough times no longer mattered. His funeral and all the arrangements were a breeze because Dad had everything organized from his pallbearers, to his music, to all his business matters. He had planned and handled every detail. That was my dad. Max and I just had to show up. Some of his family, old work associates, and his AA buddies attended. He was loved. And he loved.

Back at his house, we found all his belongings organized. His closet was sorted by color and item. His desk was immaculate. His checkbook was balanced to the penny. That was my dad. We donated most of his belongings except his books and a few clothing items. I got his AA medallions and the coffee cup he made in treatment at Valley Hope.

The death of my dad brought forth several emotions I did not know I had inside…guilt, grief, and a profound sense of loss. Most people never knew what I was feeling because all my life I had worked to be energetic and happy and positive on the outside. It was getting harder to keep my pain bottled up.

The hardest thought for me to confront was that I could not save my dad. Though I tried, I could not help him stop drinking. I knew I was his "chosen one," as Mom and Max would say, but I could not make him stay sober. It haunted me that he died alone, drinking. Over time, I found I couldn't stop thinking about his death and the bottles the police officers cleared away; it weighed on me more. When I went on long runs, I would sometimes need to stop and sob, bent over crying and trying to catch my breath with tears streaming down my face because I was never talented enough to cry and run for any distance. Like so many others grappling with grief, I cried out to God, "Why?"

I ran longer distances and worked out more than ever to cope with the many shades of my grief, but it wasn't enough. I worked harder and longer at work, too. That seemed to help. In actuality, it was a distraction, but I liked to think this was healthy and helping me get through.

Then came the first sign I was not handling my life so well.

I was sitting in the board room at work when I started to feel like I could not get enough oxygen with each breath. Then, it was happening throughout the day, every day. It didn't matter if I was finishing a run or in the middle of a meeting. I had to pull hard to get a full breath, and it was getting worse.

I went to the doctor, and he gave me a few tests. He asked me to breathe into the tube and raise the ball. I thought it was exercise-induced asthma; it wasn't. The doctor came back in the room with another doctor and asked me if my life had changed dramatically in the last few months. I said "No, business as usual." They blinked at me.

"Wait," I said.

"Yes," I said, "My father died in June from alcoholism." They shared a knowing look and left the room. When the doctor returned, he was holding a paper test. You may know where this is going, but I didn't. *Over the past two weeks, have you...been feeling nervous, anxious, or on edge? Not been able to stop or control worrying? Had trouble relaxing? Become easily annoyed or irritable? Felt afraid as if something awful might happen?* I checked a bunch of boxes and sure enough, I had anxiety.

Great. Just great.

The doctor said he was going to prescribe medicine. No, I thought. I do *not* want medicine. I do *not* want to have anxiety. I left the doctor's office.

"So, there you have it," I thought to myself. "I'm crazy." I was opposed to medication and in denial about having anxiety, so I ignored the doctor's advice and kept gasping for air. Ray's dad, Dr. Kempthorne, an amazing man and retired physician, told me I should take it. He said I wouldn't need to take it forever. So, I did. And consequently, I could breathe.

My first normal breath was a sigh of relief.

A few weeks later, I let out another sigh of relief and joy. We were pregnant! My dad in heaven delivered.

Finding out I was pregnant brought me joy mixed with caution. I had already been through two miscarriages and an ectopic pregnancy, so as much as I felt excited by the idea of a healthy baby, I was worried. We wanted this sweet child very much. Ray and I were on year seven of trying and did not know if it was ever going to happen. We kept our happiness and hope between the two of us. I thought, "Dad up there in heaven, do your work!"

The next few months were "open eating season" for me. It's not an exaggeration to say I ate everything in sight. The first few weeks I had morning sickness, but that did not slow me down. My team at work came to know two things. First, meetings may be moved to the employee cafeteria for me to graze while we worked. Second, Scott Bargman, the facilities manager, told me my team was catching on to me not remembering everything. Hmmmm. So, with that little tidbit of news, I started writing things down. Love that man!

I bloomed from a size 6/8 to 200 pounds, a total gain of 62 beautiful (not so much) pounds. I ate every turkey sandwich made in Kansas City and bought peanut butter chocolate ice cream cones from Baskin-Robbins every day. One day, I walked into the Baskin-Robbins on 87th Parkway in Lenexa and the counter girl told me they were out of peanut butter chocolate ice cream. I literally started crying. I felt sorry for the young girl working there, but not as sad as I felt for me. I got in the car and drove directly to the nearest Baskin-Robbins on Shawnee Mission Parkway—10 minutes away. I walked in with purpose…and *they* had my ice cream. Girl.

After my daily ice creams, next to nothing fit. I had one pair of black pants and a few jackets I rotated through for work. My undergarments could have been used as a mast for a small ship. Pregnancy did not look flattering on me and all my chins.

We did not know if we were having a boy or a girl. We wanted a surprise. For a girl, we leaned toward Maria (for Miep) and Ann (my mom's middle name). We had two names we loved for a boy: Case, after Ray's Uncle Om Kees in the Netherlands, and McKinley, after Ray's grandfather Guy McKinley. But little Case McKinley was not feeling the need to be birthed. A few days after I was due, I was induced.

On June 12, 2001, I packed up my suitcase and headed to Shawnee Mission Medical Center with Ray to start the induction. This child was quite comfortable and found no need to enter the world, even after 10 hours. My brother and Ray's dad were sent home from the hospital after our doctor told us the baby was not coming. Well, this strong-willed woman was told I *was* having a baby that day, so I let every medical person who entered our room know the baby was coming out. Around 6 p.m. (without the Pitocin) my water broke, and, by the grace of God, I got an epidural. Out came the most beautiful little man I had ever laid eyes on. Case McKinley Kempthorne was born at 7:53 p.m. and weighed 8lbs, 7oz. The moment the doctor placed Case in my arms, I knew love, real love. It was the love my parents had for me, and the love our Father, Jesus Christ, has for us.

I know those of us who have children could write an entire book about these little people. I am no different. Though Case was eight years in the making and came 60 pounds later for me, this little man was worth every tear shed and every pound gained.

God had blessed his father and me to parent, love, and watch over this child. We cried the minute we saw Case: tears of thanksgiving, tears of pain that my father and Ray's mother would never hold him, and tears of joy for the immense love I felt for the first time in my life.

Being a mom has made me a better person. I can see the unwavering love of Christ in the way I love Case. I am more patient, more centered, and more forgiving. Case grounded me. I now have a huge appreciation for all the parents and grandparents who juggle so much, especially single moms and dads.

Being a mother is the hardest job I will ever have, but more rewarding than any other work I can imagine. Even during the first weeks of having a newborn when there is no such thing as sleep, the Terrible Twos, Threes, and the occasional eye-rolling of a teenager, I loved it and I embraced the ways it changed me. I went from being a sharp dresser at work to suiting up with spit up stained shirts and mismatched shoes. Case was an extremely easy child to parent. Who puts himself in timeout when he's three years old?

Three months after Case was born, September 11, 2001 shook our country.

For those of us alive on 9-11, most of us remember where we were the moment we learned the twin towers were hit and the third plane went missing in Pennsylvania.

"The World Stopped Turning," as Alan Jackson sang in his famous song.

I was on the exit to Armour Road in North Kansas City when the radio DJ suddenly went off the air. I drove up to the parking lot at work, walked into the employee dining room, and watched the TV. I was struck with horror as I watched the towers fall. As an executive, I knew I had to go upstairs and group with the others on the Executive Team. This was much bigger than us. Inside, I wanted to go home and hug my family and my newborn son.

The executives huddled in an office and made our plan. We were able to send employees home as we had no guests. My team cut the majority of our staff for the remainder of the day. The FAA landed all planes in the U.S., and we had work to do as a hotel casino. Along with all other hotels in the Kansas City areas, we worked with the Convention and Visitor's Bureau to create a pool of hotel rooms for travelers grounded in the KC area.

At home, September 11 brought another complexity. Ray and I had decided to pursue working with an au pair agency so I could go back to work full time. After searching and reading numerous au pair applications and referrals, reviewing background checks, and conducting phone interviews, Ray and I met an amazing young woman from Cobourg, Ontario, Canada. Melissa was perfect for our family with years of experience with small children. We were so excited!

Melissa was in au pair training in New York when the towers fell. We didn't know if she was okay or where she was. I was sure her parents back in Cobourg were thinking there was no way they would let their daughter stay in America during a time like this.

I needed to be at work longer that day than I liked; we had to stay plugged in to corporate to offer support and be ready if other of Harrah's locations needed help. I went home late that night. On my drive home, I finally broke down crying. I was scared and sad and lost. How could anyone do anything so heinous? What was going to happen tomorrow? When I walked inside, I picked up Case and held him tight. My mom and husband were there, and Max joined us. With the rest of America, we were stunned into silence and watched the news flash by on TV.

Each day after that was a new normal in America. My little piece of the world—my neighbors, coworkers, and family—looked at others with both immense love for humankind and a little fear of the unknown. Life for everyone in the United States would be different forever. But one thing was for sure, America pulled together as a country. Red, white, and blue flags flapped in front of every business and home in town. We were proud to be American, and a sense of patriotism and love pulsed through our town.

Melissa made it from New York to Lenexa via planes, trains, and automobiles. We picked her up at the train station in Kansas City many days after her anticipated arrival, but she was safe.

Within the next year, my casino journey would take me to St. Louis, where I went "backward" to go forward. Harrah's asked me to move to St. Louis for two reasons—to learn slot operations (the bread and butter of the casino industry) and to see if my leadership skills held up outside of Kansas City. I had grown at Harrah's North Kansas City under the tutelage of the "Joann Hauser umbrella," and it was time for me to do it on my own—or so my division president said. So, off we all went—me, my husband, my son, my au pair Melissa, and our German short-hair dog, Chas.

I transferred to Harrah's St. Louis as the assistant director of slots—an assistant. Harrah's was going to pay me to learn. I sat in one of my first meetings and unintentionally made it clear I had no idea what I was doing in the world of slot operations. In a meeting held in the executive conference room, leaders met to discuss internal controls (the accounting and auditing processes that casinos follow to ensure that financial reporting meets laws and regulations). As important as internal controls is in any business, it's an uber big deal in the casino world because a large portion of revenue goes back to the state in the form of tax dollars.

In that meeting, one leader brought up an "EGD," and soon everyone in the conference room was discussing the "EGDs." As a past hotelier and leader of valet services, security, and the like, I had no idea what the executives were talking about… and it seemed like the "EGDs" were a big deal. So, I asked what an EGD was.

Everyone in the board room turned and looked at me. I knew my question must have been really stupid. "Electronic Gaming Device. Dawn, those are your slot machines." Lordt, I thought.

I am sure these leaders were wondering what sort of casino executive the division president had sent them. Yes, I had a lot to learn.

Once again, the Lord showed up in my work…blessing me with an education from one of the most amazing, beautiful Christian ladies in the business: Xenia Wunderlich. Xenia, who was from Northern Nevada, was a kind, soft-spoken lady with long blonde hair and beautiful nails. She was rarely flustered, but when she was, you knew it. She was like the mother you never wanted to let down–with kind words and a heart for everyone.

While in St. Louis, I learned slot operations–gaming math, slot floor layouts, purchasing of slot machines, and slot service from Xenia and two men who are still in the industry: Jay Snowden, now the CEO of Penn Gaming, and David Patent, CEO of VizExplorer. Jay and David, both Harvard grads, are great guys and crazy smart. While David worked at our corporate offices, Jay's office was next to mine in St. Louis. I learned a great deal from him, even though I was nearly old enough to be his mother. Jay was wise beyond his years, respectful—but with crazy high standards—humble and funny. In the years since I worked under Jay, I've worked with a few bullies and narcissists. I so often wished they could spend a week with Jay learning how to act as a leader. I absorbed as much as I could from Xenia, Jay, David, and the team of managers, supervisors, and employees in slots. They knew the business like no one else. How could you not love a team that could fix a slot machine, schlep a 50 pound bag of coins across the casino, and entertain a guest when the music was loud and the casino bells were even louder?

As there often is in the casino world, my team had a general manager change, and the leadership team changed a bit as well. After just a few months, I was tapped to be the vice president of human resources. I was honored. It was one of my favorite positions in my 20+ years in the business, and I would never have gotten it if I'd turned down the chance to take a lower position in St. Louis. If you are trying to move up in a company, sometimes you have to go backward to go forward. There is no way I could immediately start leading the strategy of a department where I flat out did not understand the basics. But with patience, I had learned and managed to take a leap forward in my career.

Human Resources is where I knew God wanted me to be. To encourage, train, and support the hearts of thousands of employees in gaming.

During this period of my career, I was frequently asked if it was tough to be a woman in gaming. People want to know if it's a man's world and whether I was paid fairly in comparison to my male colleagues.

I never had a problem with pay equity or the glass ceiling. In the early '90s and 2000s, there were more men in top positions than women, especially on the gaming side: slots and table games. But over the course of my career, women moved into top positions including Vice President, Senior Vice President, General Manager, and Division President, myself included.

Because casinos work when people play, some women in the '90s and 2000s had to make the choice between being a mommy and working every holiday. On Christmas, Thanksgiving, Easter, the Fourth of July, and especially New Year's Eve, casino employees and their leaders work. (At least they ought to! How can you ask your employees to work a holiday when you're at home?)

Early in my career, I attended slot summits where most of the leaders in the room were men, but I was not intimidated in the least. I never worried about what I was getting paid in relation to my male peers, but most of the time, I didn't know how much they were making. When I became the VP of HR, I did come to know the salaries. I am not going to say that I didn't ever see a salary of a new executive guy and shake my head—because I did—but I moved on. Quite frankly, I negotiated my salary, and that was on me. If I wanted a higher salary, then I had to produce.

I was blessed to work for and around many amazing female leaders. Joann Hauser, of course; Marilyn Winn Spiegel, Xenia Wunderlich, Robbie Bulter, and Ginny Shanks just to name a few. Working with those women taught me so much about myself.

These women could be firm, yet have genuine empathy, be crisp, polished, and brilliant and yet have caring perseverance—not having to "prove" themselves at the expense of others. I knew that if I could help people be their best, personally and professionally, my employees could win and so could Harrah's. This is where God wanted me at the time, learning the leadership lessons that would guide me through the rest of my career.

In less than two years, I was tapped again for a new position back in operations—a position that was especially alluring because it was a promotion and would bring me home to Kansas City. I was offered vice president of operations (assistant general manager) at Harrah's North Kansas City. The nice thing about my career at this time is that the division president asked me about my thoughts and desires for my career along with what was best for me and my family. It doesn't get better than that. These leaders also asked if I wanted to go back and get my MBA or if I wanted to move to Joliet, Atlantic City, and other cities across the country. My husband and I talked it over and decided to return to Kansas City. So, off the family and our new au pair Steffi went.

There's no place like home!

Though it was nice being near where my sorority sisters, my brother, and my mom lived, moving back into operations took some rewiring.

In St. Louis, the hours had been varied and long but more regular than what I'd experienced elsewhere in casinos. The human resources work had been very conducive to being a new mommy. In operations, I was back to working every holiday and weekend. Though my 3-year-old son had no idea what day it was, I still felt bad. I did not make it home every night for dinner. Sometimes I wouldn't even make it home to put Case to sleep. I was finding it hard to make it to church on Sunday because I wasn't getting home from work until 1 a.m.

On top of struggling to contain my work schedule, my anxieties and worries started to pile up. The pressures of work were coming home with me each evening, which is a lot to add to the obvious stresses of being a new parent. The haunting reminder of not being able to save my dad waned in and out, interrupting my thoughts day and night. I had worked at Harrah's North Kansas City when he had passed away, and I was back. I wished that he could see my son and my successes. I still wished I could have saved his life.

Two or three glasses of wine at night seemed to ease the craziness in my life and my head. I wasn't up to a bottle yet, but I was using alcohol to ease my stress and pain. To avoid the troubles inside my head, I poured myself into my work. While I was still going to church almost weekly with the family, my heart wasn't in it. It was hard to tell from the outside, but I was moving further from God and my relationship with Christ. I could place blame on a lot of external factors, but ultimately my increased drinking and distance from my faith was all on me. I had the job, the title, the house, the cars, the trips, the au pairs, a healthy, beautiful son, and husband…but it was not enough. Lord, how did I not see what I was doing while I was doing it? I was self-destructing.

At one point, I drove myself to church and walked into the counselor's office. I shared *everything* with a pastor and a counselor, sobbing the whole time. I was in so much pain, crying out for help. We prayed, but the pain did not stop. Work did not stop, and life did not stop. On top of everything, my marriage was crumbling. I was imploding.

In the middle of it all, I was offered a big promotion in Las Vegas as the corporate vice president of training for the entire company. My husband and I talked about the move. We decided to go; we actually thought the move might help our marriage.

CHAPTER 9

And Sometimes You Just Wander

Have you ever been at church, listening to the pastor's sermon, and you swear that God had these words written and spoken just for you? This has happened to me nearly every week at church for my whole life. Many times, I get a nudge from my husband or son when they know I'm working the sermon over in my head, connecting to the words. It is as if God is speaking quietly right to me. And He is.

One recent Sunday, my preacher Chip spoke my story, which he often does. He spoke my "wandering" and "Promised Land" story to the tee! Each of us are somewhere on the timeline from Egypt to Babylon.

We are all somewhere on the road from Egypt to the Wilderness to the Promised Land, or the goal of our journey. In his sweet Southern drawl, the pastor explained that Egypt represents bondage and sin—when we are not in a relationship with Christ. Wilderness is a time of "testing and training," in which we are training to trust God. After some time in the Wilderness, we give our self and our life to Christ and decide to live His will in the Promised Land. The Promised Land is still full of "battles and blessings" where we fight battles, yet are blessed with God's provision, protection, and presence. Life is not always easy, but you overcome. Then there is the "time out" of Babylon. The time spent in Babylon is a place of removal until we repent from our sins in the journey to get back to God's many blessings in the Promised Land.

Moses wandered for more than 40 years in his trek to take Israel to the Promised Land of Canaan. At times, Moses questioned his own ability to lead more than 600,000 people out of the wilderness. Joshua too. God inflicted pain and suffering when his people continually chose to ignore him. But still, like me, they are humans and think they know best, which is why they end up with "plagues, storms, starvation and the rest." If we would just listen to Him.

My life from 2006 to 2010 mimicked Babylon for me. After having lived in the Promised Land, I needed to repent and get back to God's will for my life.

I had perfected wandering and was completely lacking in obedience. I was truly ready for God's will in my life. When my life eventually synced up to God's will, I saw the provision and promises of God like no other. In the end, his grace showed out! But ohhhh, the journey to align myself with God's will was a long and hard one.

Home to big names, big casinos, big money, amazing food, and even more amazing shopping, some might think that Las Vegas would be the "Promised Land." Others say there is no way they could live in Las Vegas. All in all, Las Vegas is a great place to live. I did not raise my son on the Strip. We lived among churches, stores, schools, and great trails to run and walk on. It wasn't just bright lights and loud buildings; the beautiful Red Rock Mountains are right outside town, and we could go skiing at Mount Charleston, less than an hour away. I met some of the most amazing, brilliant, life-changing people during my time living there.

But Lord help me, Las Vegas was not easy for me.

My marriage had dissolved. We somehow believed that the move to Las Vegas would help.

Within months of moving, we were separated...and then eventually divorced. My marriage to Case's dad, Ray, was mostly a wonderful journey. It takes two to make a marriage work, and it takes two to make it dissolve. I definitely own my part of the divorce, eventually making amends with Ray (and with Case when he was old enough).

Once I moved to Las Vegas, I had poured myself into my new position at Harrah's. I was the corporate vice president of HR training for the entire company. I worked with insanely smart people, learned from the best in many industries, and had the opportunity to make a difference for thousands of people and my company. Having an office at Caesar's Palace on the Strip was pretty cool, too. Restaurant options were endless (though the employee cafeteria was just like a casino buffet and much cheaper), and I loved to go shopping at the Forum Shops after work. But then I began making a habit of having a couple glasses of wine with my girlfriends after a tough day at the office. A couple glasses of wine could turn into an expensive shopping spree with Louis Vuitton, Dolce & Gabbana, and countless other stores just steps away.

Casino employees know that "normal" hours means weekends and holidays—we work when people play. In Vegas, I was at corporate which meant I had more regular hours. I was traveling, too, for weeks at a time. Not only within the U.S., but abroad.

Around that time, our CEO asked me to write a training program for senior executives throughout the brand to experience the growth and innovation of the gaming sector in Macau, an administrative region of China. Our goal was to help these leaders experience the "out of the box" thinking that had been so successful in the city. It was an amazing, daunting task but rewarding. I was blessed to lead an executive development team that lived in various parts of the world including Macau, Hong Kong, and Las Vegas. Our goal was to invite top leaders from all over the world to travel to Macau, stay in the hotels, eat in the restaurants, see what the culture had to offer, and understand how this translated back into U.S.-based operations. Gaming was growing all over the world and our CEO wanted to ensure top leaders were abreast of what this meant to their work. I developed pre-work, a specific learning experience outline, and group projects for the participants. When the visiting executives returned to work in the States, each had to write up a synopsis of what they learned and how they could apply it to their Harrah's Entertainment team.

The trip was priceless. I traveled to Hong Kong and Macau and saw a part of gaming and culture I would have never been able to experience otherwise. I was amazed by Hong Kong's posh retail and exquisite food. I have never eaten so many meals without knowing what I was eating. I had sea urchin with the spines still attached more than a few times, but it was delicious. The pace of Hong Kong reminded me of New York. The skyline was beautiful, and the city was fast and happening. Everywhere we toured, people were polished, professional, and dressed to the nines. Next, we took a ferry ride to Macau. Gaming and casinos were the heart of the region, and down each street people were shopping for deals. The street sellers (and back rooms) hawked knock-off Louis Vuitton, Chanel, and Rolex. Personally, I enjoyed the shopping!

To this day I cannot believe that I joined many in our tourist group in jumping off the Macau Tower. The tower, an iconic part of the Macau skyline, stands 1,109 feet tall and looks like a much taller, much glassier version of Seattle's Space Needle. Our guides walked me to the edge of the building's jump area, gear already on, and slowly locked me into the safety equipment with my tandem jump partner, another woman executive I worked with. A lump rose up in my throat and my heart raced as I looked across Macau. Then I made the mistake of looking down. I semi-smiled at the camera man taping our jump, told Case I loved him through the video, and jumped. I am not sure if I would have done it without someone by my side. Either way, I did it and can check that off my bucket list (though I'm not sure it was on my bucket list to begin with)!

With job promotions in the entertainment industry came more perks like the Macau trip. I attended elegant dinners and went on more luxurious trips. I flew in private planes and rode in limousines for work. Most trips landed me in luxury hotels with exquisite meals that were events all by themselves. I had VIP access to clubs, where I met and partied with celebrities.

Meeting famous people is a norm in the gaming and entertainment world. From actors and singers, to all-star athletes and business moguls, many of them end up at a casino. Some of the most famous people I've met are humble, kind, and generous. But other celebrities have been very arrogant and demeaning. Those of us in the entertainment industry know that the singer who's a "ding dong" at one casino is generally a "ding dong" everywhere else, too. You have to give them kudos for being consistently high maintenance and picky. But one thing holds true of the most famous of the famous—those A-listers at the upper echelons of fame. They are humble and never forget where they came from. Case in point: Garth Brooks.

I had the opportunity to spend time with Garth Brooks when he visited our casino in North Kansas City. He was one of the nicest gentlemen I have ever met in my personal or professional life. On his visit to our casino, he spent hours stopping and visiting with *every* guest who wanted to chat. When he asked about their families and lives, it was with genuine interest and care.

He especially loved hearing people talk about their children. Our guests loved it. The only problem was it was hard to keep him on time for his scheduled appearances.

Other notable kind stars are Si, Jep, and Jessica from Duck Dynasty. Jep and Jessica spoke about taping Duck Dynasty and patiently answered every little question we had about how production works. And Si...he was just as much of a wonderfully hot mess in real life as he is on TV. As wild as he seems, he was incredibly polite and interactive with the guests. The kids were enamored with him as he bent down to their level to chat. And he showed up to dinner at a Phillip M's restaurant at Pearl River Resort with his jug of tea in hand. The real deal. During dinner (after Jep and Si had left to be with guests), Jessica opened up to me about how she works to keep "normalcy" in her children's life.

I have met and spoken with other beautiful musicians, actors, and athletes. The boxer Evander Holyfield and Angel's baseball player Albert Pujols are both kind men. I spent no more than 30 seconds with Tim McGraw, but he is a favorite of mine. I remember a time in New Orleans when I walked up to a group of executives before one of our dinner business meetings. We were standing in an elegant, dark restaurant bar talking among ourselves while we waited for our room to be ready. Ladies and men alike stood in their snappy business suits, but I noticed one man was not in business attire. As a matter of fact, he was in jeans and a short-sleeve shirt. He was laidback and kind, but couldn't have cared less about what he was wearing. After a minute, a division president introduced me to him. No wonder he was in a Hawaiian shirt; it was Jimmy Buffet.

There are performers who I only needed 30 seconds with to know that they were anything but gracious. At one performer's meet-and-greet, she was incredibly rude and told us to get the guests in and out as quickly as possible. *What?* She was being paid to visit with our guests as well as perform. I couldn't believe she wanted to rush her fans in and out. She could barely force a smile for each photo. I loved her before I met her, but when I was driving home after her event that day, I flung her CD out the car window. Other performers were the same way. My son knows who's cool and who isn't. After concerts and shows, he always wanted the skinny on how they acted and what special requests they made on their riders. Did they want special foods or make requests for bizarre snacks or drinks?

These famous people are merely people, with hearts and souls like ours. Some are nice, and others not so much. Regardless, I was paid to accommodate them so that they would entertain our guests. And I did it, even if I was struggling not to roll my eyes at times.

Add in dating to the luxurious lifestyle, and I was a hot mess. Sure, I was "living the life," but deep inside I hurt. I had great clothes, purses, shoes, and nice cars. I was self-soothing with all these worldly things, trying to show myself and the world I was "enough" by surrounding myself with more and more stuff. My identity was wrapped up in my career, my belongings, and validation from others. It was a recipe for disaster.

By 2007, my investments started looking rough. I remember opening my quarterly updates on our money: It looked like a graph headed southeast—in red.

And then came 2008.

Harrah's had purchased Caesar's Entertainment and the new company was looking at "economies of scale"—the cost advantage of having a larger business. Like many organizations at the time, Harrah's was trying to use mergers and acquisitions to do more with less. Our day-to-day culture began to feel very different from the days when it had just been Promus and Harrah's. It had moved from "The Better People Place" to margin management central. I thrive in environments where we need to continually look for ways to work "faster, better, and stronger" and understand their necessity, but they never work when it is at the expense of the company's environment and the people who work there.

Reductions in force (layoffs) happen. I have seen (and overseen) it done quickly and mercifully, like ripping off a Band-Aid, and I have watched it done poorly, with people losing their jobs day after day after day while stress and uncertainty grows among those still working. Not only does productivity tank, anxiety goes through the roof.

My mentors had always taught me that every casino has pretty similar slot machines, tables, hotels, and restaurants. It is the people and their service that differentiates and creates the experience that attracts and retains customers.

Case in point: Chick-fil-A. Many restaurants sell chicken, but no one sells chicken with a smile and heart like Chick-fil-A. Their revenue continues to point to that success.

The economy was shaky, and the company had just made a purchase that made us the largest gaming company in the world. Then in early 2008, Harrah's Entertainment went private. The Caesar's acquisition left the company with even more moving parts and a lot of tough decisions to be made.

And then in August of that year, I lost my job.

Christine Rury was my dear friend from North Kansas City, and had become a fellow vice president in Vegas. One day, she asked to meet me at a Biaggi's for lunch. Rury (as we all call her to this day) was vague about why we were meeting. It didn't sound like a routine "friend" lunch. Though we were best friends, I sensed that something bad was about to happen.

I met Rury in the restaurant, which was one of my favorites, and we sat down across from each other at a booth. Sure enough, she handed me a packet: my severance package. Time slowed. The room, so beautiful and ornately decorated and busy with lunch chatter a minute ago, now seemed silent and empty to me. My position was being eliminated.

What was this happening to me? My reviews had been amazing for decades. But it turned out that in the wake of mergers and cutting margins, my performance didn't matter anymore. Harrah's was all about business, and I was not going to be a part of it any longer. The severance package was great, but I wanted to work. Harrah's Entertainment was all I knew and loved. That job was the biggest of all the worldly possessions I had been collecting. That job, my foundation, was gone.

I went back home that day and sat alone in my humongous house with a glass of wine. That glass became a bottle, which then became several more. I told no one for days. Not my friends, not my brother, and definitely not my son or mother.

I had absolutely no idea what to do next. Losing my beloved career took away the greatest distraction I had from the immense sadness I had been hiding from. Still unable to face my inner turmoil, I soothed myself with more wine, and told myself that what I needed was to find a job. I really needed more than that. I needed help.

It was getting harder for me to hide this chaos from Case. Today, he says he remembers very little of this time of our lives. Looking back, this chaos of wandering was just five years of my life—10% of my time on this Earth—but it aged me 10 years.

Sally, our German au pair, came with us from Kansas City to Las Vegas. She blessed our lives during the move and continued to afterwards. Sally skipped when she walked and her reddish-blonde hair, thin frame, big beautiful smile, and sweet German accent filled our house with joy. Sally was always positive, always on time, and always present. Her smile, organization, energy, and grace had been ever-present in our lives since 2005 and would stay in our lives forever—not as our au pair, but as our cousin. Sally eventually married my cousin's child, Brian Bachman, after they met at my Aunt Judy's funeral in Pleasanton, Nebraska. In Las Vegas, Sally would receive her bachelor's degree in mechanical engineering from UNLV. Sally was always incredibly smart and tenacious. She and Brian now have two beautiful girls, Klara and Maja. God is good like that! Our lives never missed a beat during this time thanks to Sally. God gave me Sally. That I know.

Case and I had started attending Central Christian Church in Las Vegas. That church is a light in a murky world for many. Jud Wilhite, the senior pastor, is a man that I watched bring many people to Christ. The megachurch welcomed everyone: the rich, the homeless, the broken, the weak, and the sick. If ever you visit Las Vegas, it is a must-see service. It has been described as a Cirque du Soleil production with worship, praise, and thousands of hands risen to the Lord. At Christmas, we have had drummer boys and performers coming out of the ceiling. And it all seemed to be a natural part of church. I know this is not for everyone, and that is okay.

Case and I went to church every week. I took copious notes in service while Jud spoke. Tears frequently streamed down my face. Sitting alone was not a problem for me because it was my "me time" with the Lord.

I soon felt the desire to be in a community with people like me. Like many churches throughout the country, Central Christian has small groups that meet regularly outside of church to study the Bible and build fellowship among believers. Though I was broken, I knew joining a small group was what I needed to do. One day at a church meet-up, I volunteered to host a small group at my house in Henderson. Case and I loved to entertain. What better way was there to serve others on a weekly basis than by opening our house to fellowship? I knew that God could, and would, save me from my chaos; I just needed be in the Word.

My journal during those years is so difficult for me to read today. Some days have scripture verses and notes from church service. Those were the days when I was putting in the work to get deeper in my faith. Other days, the pages are filled with the words of a lost, broken girl. I was depressed, having trouble sleeping, and experiencing uncontrollable binge eating each night. Soon, I was seeing every doctor I could—my OB/GYN, my psychiatrist, and an internal medicine doctor who referred me to a sleep clinic to learn how I could get a good night's rest.

My head was never calm and constantly full of insanity. How did I get to this point? Where was the simple, care-free, hard-working Dawn from Kansas? How could life spin out to the point where I was incapable of rest and reflection?

The saddest journal entries are full of faint, barely legible scratches: "Still night eating. I must conquer this before I try to diet. I ate a sandwich last night and wasn't hungry. I couldn't stop. 12:30 a.m."

Another entry reads, "Up at 1:30 a.m. and 2:30 a.m. I wasn't hungry, but I did it anyway." The words taper off to nothing.

One doctor prescribed me sleeping pills. I tried them for a few nights but woke up as I ran into a wall, breaking a picture hanging in front of my bed. When Case came in the next morning, he was puzzled. Believe me, so was I. Besides, I knew sleeping pills were not going to work for me as a single mom. I needed to be able to wake up on the fly in case something was wrong. And beyond that, I knew that sleeping pills were only treating the symptom of a larger issue. If I actually wanted to change my life, I had to look within.

On May 10, 2009, Case and I went to church like we did every week. I got up, made our breakfast, and had a cup of coffee. I was wearing my tie-dye blue sundress. One of the beautiful aspects of Central Christian was that no one cared what anyone wore: sundresses, shorts, jeans, t-shirts. It always felt very comfortable, even if a person or family wanted to dress up. Central Christian is a church accepting of everyone, regardless of appearance.

That particular Sunday, Case and I happened to bring his best friend, Jack McNeil. Jack lived across the street and was his first friend in Vegas. They were practically twins: both very kind and smart, avid readers and members of chess club. Sweet little boys by all accounts.

Jack's mom, Carie, is one of the best friends God could have gifted me. Since becoming friends, Carie and I have entertained ourselves with our marathon conversations during play dates, drank wine together (though she didn't have a problem), ran and swam laps together, and even traveled together. Her husband, Ian, is just as special as Carie, and one of the brightest men I have ever met. Carie is a few years younger than me, naturally beautiful with her flowing brunette hair, big brown eyes, huge smile, and sweet Canadian accent. Carie never needs to wear makeup, and her athletic figure is perfect in every outfit she throws together. She could make a flour sack look amazing! Gorgeous as she is, Carie's soul and spirit far outshine her external beauty. Her philanthropic heart and hands are visible through the impact they have had on her friends, family, and groups that needed support. People love to be around Carie and Ian.

I had no inkling that this Sunday at church would be different from any other. Jack and Case went off to Sunday school and I attended the service.

Jud was preaching about salvation and grace (a frequent topic at Central Christian). He was the first pastor I had who preached like a pastor but looked like the guy down the street with his schoolboy haircut and preppy glasses. He wore a t-shirt and jeans to lead services, and when he spoke to his congregants, he spoke to us as the complex people we were: broken yet forgiven. As much as I cried during his services, I also found myself laughing at his jokes and stories. He preached the Word, spoke about the Dallas Cowboys, his family, and his slobbery bulldog Roxy. He was also the first preacher I'd ever heard speak openly about being in alcohol recovery. He always seemed to speak to me.

On that Sunday, Jud told us, "It's okay to not be okay, but you don't need to stay there." He invited to the front of the church those who wanted to give themselves to Christ and be baptized *that day*.

I had been baptized as an adult in Topeka, but I still did not have a relationship with Christ. Today was the day to commit. I walked down in front of the congregation and prayed with hundreds of others about accepting Christ as our Lord and Savior. Tears of joy streamed down my face as thousands of others watched.

Case and Jack came out of Sunday school, and I told them I was going to get baptized. Those two were not a bit surprised. We were living in Vegas, and weirder stuff happened all the time.

The three of us walked outside where the large pools were set up in the parking lot with pastors ready to baptize. No detail was overlooked. There was a sign-up area, a place to pick up a dry shirt, stacks of towels, and a bin for wet clothes. Hundreds of people got baptized that day. I went up the ladder, down into the water, and gave myself to Christ, right there in my tie-dyed blue sun dress in an above-ground pool smack in the center of a church parking lot in Las Vegas.

I was no longer going to live in fear, shame, and rejection. I was new again in Christ! I was finally enough.

Over the course of the next year, starting with that baptism, I started to get my life in order. Only through my relationship with Christ and my amazing friends and family could this *ever* have happened. In just a few months, I would take my last drink.

I began drinking to become numb back in high school and kept it up through college. I drank just as much as my friends and sorority sisters, but some days I drank to forget. By the time I moved to Kansas City my drinking wasn't excessive by any stretch, but it was becoming my main tool to relax and forget. By the time I got to Las Vegas, I wasn't drinking every day, but there were days when one bottle of wine wasn't even close to enough.

The weekend I took my last drink began like an average weekend in Las Vegas. Carie, Ian, and I went to a pool party for a friend's birthday. Beautiful people in swimsuits lounged along the edge of a pool that was gorgeous enough for a Ritz-Carlton Resort. There were palm trees everywhere, music, laughter, love, amazing food, and fun cocktails.

It was going to be a great celebration.

Unfortunately, it only started out great. It ended with me sitting by myself in my monster house crying. Everyone was upset and concerned for me— Carie more than anyone else. It was a blessing that Case was on his yearly visit to see his Dad in Montana for two months. At least he did not have to see this.

The day after the pool party, I called Carie. She picked up the phone and let me know that she was done watching me ruin my own life. We had ended the day at home with everyone tucked away safely, but my life was spinning out of control. Though Carie didn't want to talk to me, she had called my ex-husband Ray to get my brother's phone number.

Then came the phone call from Max. The wake-up call that I needed: "Go ahead and kill yourself just like Dad did." He hung up.

That was all he needed to say. I sat there and cried all day. Carie's beautiful mother, Carol, came over to talk to me. I remember going to my wine refrigerator and getting a bottle for us to share. We sat at the island in the kitchen and I poured her a glass to talk over. Little did I know this would be the last drink I would take to this day. My head was foggy, and it was hard to process what Carol was saying to me. She wanted me to go get help, to talk to someone. And while I had been talking to a counselor, I wasn't ready to change until that day. Carol gave me a hug and kiss on the cheek and left.

My friends were done. My family was done.

All I knew was that I was "sick and tired of being sick and tired." I got on my knees and prayed for God to save me from myself. Day turned into night. The next morning was a Wednesday and I did not drink. The same went for Thursday.

I knew that Central Christian hosted a program called Celebrate Recovery that I could go to that very week on Friday night. Celebrate Recovery is a "Christ-centered 12-step recovery program for anyone struggling with hurt, pain, or addiction of any kind." At the end of the week, I headed to Central Christian with my dad's AA Big Book in hand.

As I walked into the doors of Central Christian, though I felt scared about the unknown, I felt safe from being judged and safe from myself. I followed everyone into the sanctuary and sat in a seat like I was attending church. The beginning of the program was full of worship music, just like Sunday morning

in decades, and this joy came from within because I had a relationship with Christ. With Christ I had hope.

I started running again and finished two full marathons and a host of half marathons and road races. I trained for triathlons and my old swim team training came back to help. I still wasn't good at the flip turns, but I didn't have to worry about those when I was out in a lake.

Was everything perfect? Not by any means. But I was truly full of joy, facing my troubles and self-doubt head on instead of running away from them. Between the divorce and the down-turn in the economy, I had lost my house and a lot of money, but I was beginning to live the Promised Life as Chip would say. It was God's will I was following now, not mine. I was still having issues managing what I would later find out was a condition called Night Eating Syndrome (NES), but I was managing my stress and emotions in an otherwise healthy way for the first time in a long time.

My God Box

Somewhere in Vegas I acquired a God Box, a gift from someone in my meetings. My God Box is dark wood, about 4" wide by 3" high, and is printed with the scripture verse "Be still and know that I am God" (Psalm 46:10) surrounded by pressed purple flowers.

In this box are the prayers to God that I have written down, dated, and given to Him. No matter where I move, it sits on the vanity in my bathroom. Besides prayers, it contains a delicate gold mesh bag filled with AA coins celebrating my sobriety over the years. One of the most important chips in the bag is an AA coin for 34 years from my father's collection. It was given to him by his sponsor, Tom. Tom had cared enough for my dad to give him his coin of 34 years of sobriety. All wrapped up in that one token is the years of humility and work he gave to achieve freedom from addiction. This is how all our coins feel to each of us. From the 24 hour chip to the 50 year chip.

This box is very, very important to me. It's one of the first things I would grab in a fire.

Among the papers and coins are two prayers that I wrote while I was living in Vegas. Unlike the other carefully written notes, these two strips of paper were torn with just a few words scratched on each of them.

"Sleeping. Night Eating." Scratched on one slip

"A relationship." Written on another slip.

I will tell you now that God answered both prayers, and the answer was much better than I could have *ever* imagined.

Sleep. Night Eating.

During my last years in Vegas, my life was calm, and I was on a better path. I had settled into a routine of an AA meeting before work, a day at the office, and then time at home with Case, plus a daily workout.

At night, though, I fought bouts of insomnia. I would wake up the next morning with a faint recollection of eating in the night. Other nights, with no memory at all of what I'd done, I'd awake to bread crumbs, a knife, and peanut butter left out on the counter. It was a horrific feeling each morning to trace my steps and find I had eaten a peanut butter and jelly sandwich, crackers, or whatever was in the pantry. Every day I would start the morning with shame and disappointment.

During this time, I read as much as I could find on Night Eating Syndrome. Studies show that NES is really a psychological disorder tied to depression, anxiety, and chemical abuse. The data on NES was endless, so I knew I was not alone.

I was confused. I wasn't drinking anymore and was living a simple, happy life. Shouldn't this issue have gone away? And treating it proved to be equally confusing. How could I fight a "disorder" that only existed in my sleep? How could I have enough willpower each night to not eat, when

I wasn't even aware of what was happening while it happened? It was crazy! If I could do *anything* I put my mind to, how come I could *not* tackle this painful secret? The next few months were a string of unsuccessful treatments. I would deprive myself of food during the day, usually because I wasn't hungry from eating the night before, and then pray at night that I would sleep restfully and not eat. This went on for months and months and months.

I tried to hide it from Case and our au pair, Julia. My goal was to groggily get up and clean up my mess before they awoke. I went to a sleep clinic, but I was sent home before midnight because I couldn't fall sleep. I saw doctors, and they said it was a psych issue. So I prayed, and continued to sleep and eat each night. But my prayers were to no avail. Or so I thought.

Then, one night in October 2012, I was called back home to Kansas. My mother was very ill, and my brother and I were going to work together to care for her. Eventually, we put her house—our childhood home—up for sale and found her a nursing home. The first night I was in Hutch, I slept all night.

This could have been because of complete exhaustion. That day, I had gotten my mother into a nursing home in Buhler and stayed at a local hotel for the evening. I literally dropped onto the bed and slept through the night. I woke up and looked around, amazed. I scoured the room for crumbs, but there was nothing: no wrappers on the bed or nightstand, no food in the trash or the bathroom. I had slept all night and hadn't eaten a thing. It was the best feeling in the world. Tears flowed down my face.

The next two days I spent in Hutchinson were tied up with my mom, doctors, nursing homes, and realtors. Both nights I slept soundly and never wandered into the hall to buy food. I felt free from the chains of Vegas. Back home in Kansas, God answered my prayers. From that day on, I never unknowingly ate at night again.

A relationship.

When I wrote these words on the slip, I knew what I was asking God for. This was after my divorce, and I was in no good place for a relationship, drinking or no drinking.

I had dated, gone to clubs, and tried the online approach. I even tried Kelleher International, a dating program for executives which was said to "attract successful, affluent, educated singles who are passionate about their life." After I quit drinking, I found I was less interested in going out on dates.

Don't get me wrong, I met a couple kind, upstanding men who were involved in the community. I also met men that could not have cared less about a relationship. They wanted fun. They wanted what they thought I had: money and a great job. Heck, at this point I wasn't even sure who I was or what I stood for.

God knew exactly the relationship I needed—a relationship with Jesus Christ. That is *exactly* what I got that day in May 2009 when I gave myself to Christ at Central Christian. God "showed out and showed up" to answer my slip of paper once I began my relationship with Jesus Christ and put him first in all I did.

Day by day, my connection with Christ got stronger and stronger. I no longer tried to compare myself to all the beautiful people and shiny toys in Las Vegas. With God, I was whole. I was no longer going to live in shame. God forgave me for my sins…and still does to this day. The few years of insanity and drinking no longer defined me. I spent my time outside of work with Case, working out, in AA and Small Group meetings, in the Word, and living. For the first time, I had joy and hope in my life, boundaries in my relationships and my friends, and the opportunity to share my testimony with others. I had found my "why"—my "relationship" with God and Jesus Christ—right smack dab in the middle of Sin City.

The day that I finally looked back at the God Box and saw the "relationship" slip was the day that I knew He had me all along. I just had to find my relationship with Him first.

The years in Las Vegas were a time of true growth. I was eventually alone with my son in Las Vegas, but I never felt alone. Like Moses, I wandered a bit, got lost, got frustrated, questioned but never gave up. The Promised Land was ahead.

CHAPTER 10

The Land of Milk and Honey—Or Magnolia Trees and Chess Pie

B y now, I knew that Vegas was not the place for me. I had a wonderful corporate position at Pinnacle Entertainment helping in both HR and marketing, working with incredibly brilliant and amazing people all over the U.S., but I felt in my heart I needed to leave Las Vegas for me and for Case. I had thought about sending out resumes or even talking to my CEO about positions within the company out in the field. I reached out to a friend who had taken a new CEO job in Central Mississippi. We talked off and on about her transition to the South. Then one day, I started talking to her about her open positions. I told her that I would be interested in coming to see the property and learning more about the positions, her team, and what a move would mean for me and Case.

Case and I made a visit to Philadelphia, Mississippi, in mid-2012.

We flew into Jackson at night. A limo driver was standing at the end of the escalator with a sign that said "Case Kempthorne." That was the sweetest sign ever. My CEO friend knew how to market to her candidates: through the hearts of those who meant the most to them. Case smiled from ear to ear. Then we went outside and a stretch Hummer was waiting for us.

Case was ready to move!

We drove and drove and drove in the dark from Jackson to Philadelphia. It seemed like hours we drove in the night. I remember seeing the last of the "neon" in eastern Flowood and not seeing it again till we hit Carthage. After about an hour of driving, we came up over the hill and there, in the middle of nowhere, was The Golden Moon casino. *There* was the neon.

Case and I jumped out of the limo and checked in. He had the world's largest gift basket waiting for him on the table. Then we dropped from exhaustion.

We got up in the morning and opened the drapes. I will never forget what we saw when we opened the blinds: For miles and miles and miles, we could see nothing but trees. We looked at each other.

Sweet Case then said something I will never forget: "Mom, we must not be on Strip-side."

Come to find out, there was no Strip-side. Trees were on both sides... forever.

I interviewed and Case was given a gracious tour of the golf course, a great dinner at Phillip M's Steakhouse, and a visit to the waterpark.

We toured Philadelphia, Madison, and Brandon for homes. Case was most assured we could live in Mississippi when he saw the Apple Store and Barnes & Noble in Ridgeland. There may not have been any luxurious pools to swim in or a Rio Secco Golf Course down the road, but Case and I were in.

What most drew me to the resort was the Mississippi Band of Choctaw Indians. The Tribe is federally recognized with a population of around 10,000. In 1994, the Mississippi Band, under the vision and leadership of Chief Phillip Martin, opened the Silver Star Resort, which would eventually become Pearl River Resort in 2000.

The two casinos and two hotels were architecturally dramatic buildings, especially the Golden Moon casino that stands high and sleek among the trees in the middle of Central Mississippi. The restaurants had everything from buffets to fine dining. Geyser Falls Water Park is Disney-like, and the Dancing Rabbit Golf Club was named "The Augusta You Can Play" by *Golf Magazine*. The whole resort, smack dab in the middle of Mississippi, was incredibly laid-out and employed more than 2,000 people.

The people at the resort and the Tribe became my "Why." Their trust was hard to come by early on, as they have been burned by so many people in their history, but I found I could connect with them on many levels because of my childhood. Though our skin colors were different, our hearts were not.

Working at Pearl River Resort gave my work meaning. It was no longer about stock prices, but rather about being the best company for the employees—and for the Tribe—by funding their education and medical care and helping them carve out their future. I knew God wanted me here.

So in late 2012, I left Vegas for Mississippi. I was to be the vice president of resort operations.

I was happy to be back somewhere like Kansas, somewhere that felt simple.

Many people in both Las Vegas and Mississippi have asked, "Why in the world would you move from Las Vegas to Mississippi?" The only person I knew in the area was the casino CEO, and everything I knew about the area I had learned through our one visit and some research. Some areas in Mississippi had some of the highest obesity, poverty, and crime rates in the nation.

Mississippi seemed like the perfect place to make a difference.

So off we went.

I went ahead of Case by a couple months so he could finish the semester in Vegas. It is hard enough moving a child mid-year, but November would have been even more destabilizing for him. So I did some juggling. His father came and stayed in Las Vegas for some time, as did his old au pair and new cousin Sally. He had an au pair that he loved very much, Julia, but it was not her job to be a sole care giver of a child. This gave me time to put together a solid plan for us to move—namely, where to live and what schools to attend. I never doubted that it would come together, but I had to get to Mississippi to make it happen.

Upon arriving, I lived in the hotel resort. While you might think that free housing could be a great perk, I found it wasn't desirable to live at work. It was good for the first few weeks, as I could devote the majority of my time to being at work, learning, listening, and meeting the more than 2,000 employees. But living at work was exhausting. There were just a few of us living at the Golden Moon hotel, which had been closed since 2010 due to low business. It was eerie. The only guests were me, the new CFO, the new VP of gaming operations, and one other executive.

Case and I eventually moved into a corporate apartment outside Jackson, about an hour away. The hardest part of the move was that our German au pair Julia could not stay with us in Mississippi. Cultural Care Au Pair, our au pair agency, did not have an au pair counselor or group in Mississippi, so Julia could not stay. She was allowed to help us move and help get Case settled, but the dreaded day came when we had to take her to the airport to say our good-byes. Julia had become like a family member to Case and me. At the airport, we all cried and cried.

Eventually our dog Miles came to us from Las Vegas via airplane. Miles, a German shorthair lab rescue, was not keen on the new setting. Like Case and me, he took a little while to adjust. As a dog from Las Vegas, he tip-toed on grass for a while. Back in Vegas, he didn't have a great deal of access to grass at our home or on his walks with Julia and Case. Thunder was a completely new sound to him, and it terrified him. After he shivered, shook, and threw up during the first few storms, we had to get him medicine for his nerves. He eventually outgrew his fear, but the transition was proving to be hard on everyone, including the dog.

I enrolled Case in a wonderful private school. Jackson Academy was the answer to many of my nights of prayer in Las Vegas. I wanted a school for him where he could thrive, not only academically and spiritually, but socially and emotionally as well. Jackson Academy was exactly what I prayed for, and more.

Nestled on the edge of Jackson proper within the quaint Hyde Park-like neighborhood of Sheffield is the school's small campus with beautiful buildings, a pristine football stadium, and hundreds of children from grades K3-12. Girls in their checkered light blue and white dresses and big bows ("the bigger the bow the closer to God," so goes the saying down here) and little boys in their powder blue and white short sets. And upperclassmen boys in their ties and the girls in the plaid skirts and oversized sweatshirts. On top of academics, athletics, and the arts, JA offers chapel every other week where students of all ages are able to worship and share the word of God. Having a child in a school where group prayer is not only allowed but encouraged is a huge blessing.

Little by little, God was revealing the beauty of following His will and the rewards of living a life for Him and Jesus Christ before all others.

Just as we were settling into the comfort of our new world in Mississippi, adversity struck yet again from every direction.

First it was with sweet Case. In spring 2013, at just 11 years old, months after moving to Mississippi, Case started to have stomach pains that would both keep him from eating and sleeping. The pains started as cramps and turned into a living nightmare. Case is not quick to complain, but soon he was crying in pain. I took him to a pediatrician who was sure it was ulcers caused by the stress of moving to a new area and a new school. He was treated with medicine, and we were told to follow up. The pain worsened. In the middle of the night, while living at the corporate apartment, the sweet little fifth grade boy was in so much pain he told me he wanted to die.

How could this be happening?

My Lord, what had I done to my son?

I was praying to God, begging for help. Please heal Case. I didn't even know what he had yet, but I wanted his pain to go away.

Late one night, I knew I had to call 911 to find the nearest hospital because his pain had reached a new level. Within minutes of talking to 911, a fire truck and ambulance rounded the corner to the corporate apartment. The men assessed Case and recommended immediate transport to a hospital. They inserted a drip into his arm and rolled him into the ambulance to bring him to a hospital in downtown Jackson. I followed behind in my car.

That was one of the most horrific moments in my life. I watched my son be attended to through the window in the back of the ambulance as I followed to Batson's Children's Hospital. I would have ridden with him, but I didn't know anyone who could pick me up and didn't know of any taxi service in Jackson. Within a few hours of Case getting admitted, a doctor asked if we could go somewhere to talk. This had to be a nightmare, I thought as I walked with her. She brought me to a small office with room for only two chairs and a small table.

The doctor's words blurred together. She said that Case was indeed very sick based upon their preliminary results. They would need to do more tests. I sat with my face in my hands and cried. I looked up and asked if Case was going to live. Her response, lost in the haze of the stress of the day, was comforting yet noncommittal. The night turned into day.

Dr. Angela Shannon, an amazing doctor at GI Associates, directed Case's care while he moved in and out of hospitals. He had radioactive tests, every scan possible, and a colonoscopy. He begged and pleaded to stop drinking the chalky drink before his colonoscopy. We both cried as he tried to choke it down. Each test came back with more questions. Did he have C. diff, Crohn's disease, colitis? Each came back negative. He was losing weight rapidly. At one point he was 25 pounds down on his little grade school frame. He eventually swallowed a camera pill of some sort, but nothing brought us any answers. Case was a sick child with no way forward. This went on for months and months, and into the new school year. There were not enough hours in the day to pray and offer God my life for his. His dad came to help support him. The day he saw his dad, Case's magic smile made me cry.

Jackson Academy was incredibly supportive while we battled Case's health issues. At one point I was fighting traffic in from the casino over an hour away for one of his important appointments with a specialist. I was stuck on a two-lane road behind a chicken truck and a log truck. (Don't laugh! Both are big money, and you need chickens and paper.) I called the school office, and I will never forget Becky Clarke, the middle school administrative assistant, told me that she would clear traffic at the school, during carpool, for me to get through to pick him up. Sure enough, I pulled up at JA and there was Becky moving cars on Ridgewood Road for me to get Case. He hopped in and we made it to downtown Jackson.

Work was good to me. I had to leave early a few days to be at appointments with Case. About 10 months after it all began, I remember being at GI Associates when a battery of tests came in. Dr. Shannon said she believed she knew what Case had. Finally.

The doctor believed that Case suffered from a condition called small intestinal bacterial overgrowth (SIBO). In short, SIBO is a disorder in which the small intestine has an excess of bacteria that causes severe stomach pain, nausea, diarrhea, excessive weight loss, and malnutrition. The good news was that it was not life-threatening and could be treated with antibiotics and nutrition. Case had a diagnosis, and there was a treatment. The smile on Case's face when he heard this was full of pure joy. Thank you God! Tears streamed down my face.

God answered my prayers. All of this had taught me something, though. Just because you are a Christian does not mean you are exempt from pain.

This would become even more apparent in the upcoming months. My mindset changed from "Why me?" to "What am I supposed to be learning?" I was never mad at God. I was definitely sad, but never mad. I knew God had "this," whatever "this" was going to be.

I always tried to look for the blessing in the pain, and there was so much God provided to Case and me when he was sick. First, Case and I had amazing healthcare from Pearl River Resort. Never in my 20+ years in the casino business had I had such good healthcare. I did not have to worry that bills were piling up because most everything was covered by insurance. This time in our life could have really put us in a financial bind, but God provided.

But more importantly, the second blessing was the quality of healthcare in Jackson, Mississippi. The physicians and staff were top-notch at every hospital: UMMC, Baptist, St. Dominic, and GI Associates. Each physician was incredibly responsive and worked hard to make sure Case had immediate appointments. Every doctor at every location had all of Case's data at all times. There is no dollar value for the quality of care Case had during this time. He knew that the doctors and staff cared.

I wish that the only crisis going on in my early months in Mississippi was Case's illness, but it was not. The crazy thing is that when you fight giants "head on," you just keep your head down and fight. Much like when I raced in cross country and just ran without thinking, it was only after the insanity ended that I thought, "I really went through all that...at one time?"

But the trials were not over yet.

On Valentine's Day in 2013, I told Case I would be home late. The casino had an upscale restaurant, so I knew I'd be late helping out with the rush of couples.

The morning was normal. We all got up and got ready for school and work and I headed out the door. On the 50ish minute drive out to work that morning, I followed log and chicken trucks out through the beautiful fields. The shining sun and beautiful pine trees greeted me each day on my commute. By the time I got up to my office, which connected to the CFO office, I was ready for the day. I checked my answering machine and started playing messages.

A man's voice filled the room, drunk and angry. "Dawn Kempthorne," he growled, "I'm going to kill you and put you in a body bag and ship you back to Vegas." I've excluded some of the graphic, terrifying details of his string of threats. I sat there stiff in my seat. Scared and confused, I checked the number, but it had come through the operator.

The CFO popped in through the door between our offices. "You okay, Dawn?" I couldn't speak and played the next message.

"Dawn Kempthorne. We are going to kill you—"

The CFO left and went to get to get our boss, and she, in turn, decided to call the Chief.

Before you know it, my office was swarmed with Pearl River security, Choctaw Police, the Neshoba County Sheriff, and the Chief's personal security. I had no idea who had left the messages. The caller made it clear that he and his friends wanted me out of Mississippi.

I shared my hunch with the Choctaw Police, and they said they would investigate. The police told me it would be best to drive home while it was still daylight. I quit work early and headed home.

My mind raced on the drive home: Someone wants to murder me? Is my son safe? If the caller kills me, who's going to take care of my son? When I got home, I found I couldn't keep my head straight, literally. I kept turning each way to make sure there wasn't someone hiding in the shadows.

Case came home not long after me. "Why are you home?"

"I just decided to come home early to hang out with you," I said.

"Great!" he said. "What do you want to do since it's Valentine's Day?" Nothing that involved leaving the apartment, that was for sure. We ordered pizza and watched movies. I did my best to not let on what happened. When I got to work the next morning, I was given mace and a different car to drive for a few days. Things calmed for a while, though occasionally an investigator would come and ask me more questions. I left while it was daylight for a while.

Within a matter of weeks, I was informed that the FBI had decided to take on my case. The FBI? Because the casino was on a Native American reservation, it was considered federal ground—and death threats were a federal felony. It was a crazy, scary time made worse because I was new to the state, knew virtually no one, and was a single mom.

My main goal was to hide this from Case. He had enough on his little plate. The day that I had an FBI victim's advocate sitting in my living room was like no other. I really felt like this was all a bad dream, or someone had me on hidden camera and it was all a horrible joke. She came over to talk to me about the situation. She gave me a justice department pamphlet titled "Help for Victims of Crime" and her card. Case had already found the card of the Choctaw Police investigator, and I made up some story about a casino issue. There was no way he was going to find this business card. He knew the complexities of my work, but he was also very observant.

Case has a disease, and I have the FBI in my living room.

"What in the world have I done to me and my son?" I thought. I moved us 2,000 miles across the country for a better life, and for what? He was in and out of hospitals, and I was sitting in the living room with the FBI.

Over the course of a year, the investigation continued. Eventually I got the news that the investigation was over, and the man was penalized accordingly. A letter followed from the FBI stating the overview of the outcome and with that, the case was closed.

To this day, I still have the "Help for Victims of Crime" pamphlet in my nightstand as a reminder of what I have been through.

Case and I were missing Central Christian back in Las Vegas, and I knew how important it was for us to find another church to regularly attend. Someone in town recommended we try Pinelake Church, a large Southern Baptist church that was a few thousand smaller than our old church.

So off we went to Pinelake. Walking into Pinelake was a lot like walking into Central Christian, just on a smaller scale. Outside there was happy chatter and smiles all around. The building is hidden back on a huge open campus surrounded by pine trees that go on forever and reach to the heavens. Inside there are greeters, information areas, childcare areas, and a coffee shop. In the sanctuary, the layout was the same: a huge auditorium with comfortable chairs and a beautiful stage with big screens on both sides. Upon first sitting down, we all felt pretty much at home.

On that particular Sunday (our first visit to Pinelake), Senior Pastor Chip Henderson was preaching at the 11 a.m. service. Chip is 100% Southern: he talks lovingly of his "mama" and "daddy," has endless stories about SEC football and hunts in tree stands. His sermons are peppered with "y'all, "all y'all," and "snap."

I do not remember the details of that morning's sermon, but he got to a point in his share that floored me. He spoke out that his mama did not want him to go to the Silver Star casino—my casino at Pearl River Resort.

Yep, he said it.

Chip called out the name of my work and said that his mama would not want him to go there.

Well heck, what does that say for me? For us? I knew I worked in a controversial industry. I have fought this all my life, but I have never had my exact business called by name in a sermon, by the preacher.

I needed Chip to preach to me—to find common ground with those of us who worked at the casino and pour into us. In Vegas, it wasn't a stretch to say that many of Jud's congregants worked in casinos, strip clubs, and the brothels outside town.

We sat and listened to the rest of the sermon. Case knows me all too well and kept looking out the side of his eyes to try to read my expression. I just stared straight ahead. I tried to keep listening, but my mind wandered.

As we were walking out, I said nothing. Case, as if reading my mind, said, "Mom, I think you should give Chip another chance." How did he know that the thought of never returning crossed my mind? Either way, my middle school-age son was right; we needed to give Chip another chance. But first I needed to talk to him.

And that is exactly what I did.

The next day, I sat down and typed an email to Chip introducing myself. I told him I was a guest at his church the morning before, and that I liked the service, except...

Except the part where he was preaching out not to go to the Silver Star on a recommendation from his mama. In that email, I explained how I moved to the area from Las Vegas recently to take a job at the Pearl River Resort, home to the Silver Start Casino and Golden Moon Casino. I explained how my pastor Jud at Central Christian pastored to thousands upon thousands, and that many of us were casino employees. I went on to say I had never had my casino called out in church, and needed leaders like him to "pour into" us casino people to pastor to others. I did say I would expect his sweet mother to not advocate for him visiting the casinos.

Within two days Chip replied that he was pleased that I reached out. He wrote that his intention was not to judge my work and offered to stop by the resort to meet. He would be driving past Philadelphia anyway later that week on the way to his beloved Mississippi State. I replied that I looked forward to meeting and talking. I asked him to meet me at the Golden Moon.

A couple days later, up pulled Chip Henderson in his big ole truck to the Golden Moon valet. It seemed like a fitting ride for a preacher. Out of the truck jumped Chip with his small frame, college-boy clothes, brown hairdo, and big smile. He immediately offered his hand for a shake. Within minutes, I knew this guy was the real deal.

We exchanged pleasantries and headed up to my office on the second floor. Never in a million years would I have thought a Southern preacher would be sitting in my casino office, but God has a sense of humor. Chip and I had a cup of coffee and shared our stories.

We visited and visited. I came to find out that Chip had not shared the "Silver Star" story about his mama in any service other than the one I had attended. Chip and I truly believe it was all in the hands of God that we were to meet. He then prayed and prayed and prayed for me. I am not going to lie, I felt like he was trying to clean the cobwebs off me, and it worked.

Anyway, Chip Henderson is the real deal, Southern accent and all. Is he perfect? No, he openly shares his struggles from the pulpit in hopes of helping others. I eventually found out he knows Jud. It's a crazy small world we live in. It's all God.

After Chip and I visited, he asked for a tour of the casino. I warned him of two things…First, that I could not turn off the surveillance cameras, so he shouldn't be surprised if it got leaked. We laughed. And second, not to be shocked if he saw someone from his congregation in the resort. I think they would have both been surprised, in all reality. That would be a surveillance tape worth watching! Off we went through the casino. That day was the beginning of a friendship I respect. Chip wants the best for everyone. He especially wants everyone to have a relationship with the Lord.

To this day, our family belongs to Pinelake. We love our church. Among the many gifts which Chip has given me is Jennifer Van Norman. Jennifer worked at Pinelake for a while before moving into the business world. After I gave Chip the casino tour, he thought Jennifer and I would be perfect friends and that I would be a great fit for her bible study. As I sit here, Jennifer is still one of my dearest friends. And my dear Jennifer led me to my life-changing Small Group Bible Study, which led me to meet more women I could *never* live without. For more than five years, Jennifer, Julie Ethridge, Judy Raney, Sherree Allen, Teri Dawn Neely, Dianne Aycock, Angie Havard, and I have cried, prayed, and celebrated life together.

Thank you God for allowing me, Case, and Julia to go to that 11:00 a.m. service at Pinelake rather than the 9:15 a.m. service we go to every other week.

That was all God.

Though my life was slowly coming into my control, at work and at home, I was hit with another obstacle.

This time it was sweet Case, again.

One Saturday morning in 2014, Case came into my room crying so hard that I could barely understand him. He handed me his phone and showed me a video of him being bullied. I could not believe my eyes.

It was an end-of-year school event, and Case was on a bus sitting next to his best friend Gabe. Behind them, boys were mocking Case. Another boy taped it and put it online with caption "Kemp" and an emoji of a baby.

I was *beyond* furious. I don't know if I have ever been so mad in my life.

After he showed me the video, he ran back to his room sobbing. I could barely get him to talk. He did not want to leave his room, and he made it clear he definitely did not want to go back to school. Ever.

Case was shy, and he was the new kid. Most of the children in his school had been friends with each other for years. Their parents had been friends for decades, many of them attending grade school, high school, and college together. They had solid generational friendships. That's just the South. It's different than Kansas City, St. Louis, and definitely Las Vegas—and it was hard to break into such a close-knit community. Case was doing his best to find a way to fit into this new world.

Case did not want to talk.

I went back into my bedroom and immediately texted Case's sixth grade teacher, Shelle Pinkard, whom Case and I adored and respected. I did not care that it was Saturday. Even if it was Mother's Day or Christmas morning, this was getting handled. (Okay, maybe Christmas morning I would have waited until December 26.) I needed to talk to someone at the school. Shelle texted back immediately. I described the video to her, and she was as mad as me. She asked if I had a copy of the video. I said no. (Quite honestly, I did not know how to copy it.) But I figured it out and sent her the video.

Shelle said that she was going to contact the middle school dean. Within an hour, the dean, Matt Morgan, reached out to let me know he would be handling it.

Case told me he did not want anyone to get in trouble. He just wanted the bullying to stop.

Watching my child hurt because of the meanness of other children was a new form of pain for me. While I was seething, I had to be tender with Case. When he was ready to talk, I listened. Then we tried to understand what happened and why. We talked about how "hurt people hurt people." Case and I talked about how those boys obviously hurt inside, or they would not do this. Bullying is a family problem. There must have been something going on at those boys' homes for them to act in that manner. Case listened and cried, and we prayed a lot.

I spoke to Shelle and Matt a few times the following week. They assured me they had taken care of the situation. Much like in my HR work, I knew I could not know the specifics of how it was handled. I had gotten the names of the boys from Case. Luckily the event happened at the end of school, and Case did not have to go back to school to see the boys just yet. In the first two years of moving to Mississippi, my faith and my grit got stronger.

I knew I was in the right place with Case, but I prayed for the insanity to stop. I thought that between Case's illness, the FBI, and the bullying, we had been through enough.

But more was still to come.

Since coming to Mississippi, I had been having health problems. With everything else going on, I had ignored them. It wasn't just the allergies one fights when moving from the desert to a state full of trees. It was as though my brain and body would shut down. After working out, I would curl up into a ball with extreme headaches. I couldn't move. Eventually I was incapacitated even when I wasn't working out.

I was introduced to an amazing neurologist, Dr. Ruth Fredericks. Dr. Fredericks is the best of the best. She is highly sought after and booked for months out. But I got in and sat in the waiting room for hours. She was working every angle to get the headaches to stop, and I ended up taking anti-seizure medicine. One specific day, after laying in fetal position for a day after a workout, I could not get out of bed the next morning and my headache was beyond a migraine. I was sure I was dying. The beauty of God's timing is that Case was in Montana spending the summer with his father, Papa, Uncle, and family like he did every summer. He had no idea I was ever this sick. The next morning, I texted Dr. Fredericks, and she told me to have someone drive me to St. Dominic Hospital. She admitted me, and once I got upstairs, I was on a drip that included pain meds, which helped tremendously.

Dr. Fredericks ran tests and thought she had an answer; she was thinking West Nile. What? I wasn't entirely sure what that meant, but I did know it wasn't good. I didn't want to become a statistic. After one specific test, Dr. Fredericks stopped by my hospital room again and said I did not have West Nile. Praise the Lord! She was not sure why I was experiencing these symptoms, but she had a pharmaceutical cocktail that would alleviate the pain. Before it was all over, I was back in the hospital under the care of Dr. Fredericks to have an additional procedure done on my back to alleviate headache pain caused during testing. When the doctors flipped me over after the back procedure, my headache pain was reduced by a million. I had no idea what I had, what caused it, or what the future had in store for my noggin, but I knew that Dr. Fredericks was making my life better.

At this point into my time in Mississippi, abnormal was the new normal. I was running out of events for the circus! It was like I was being tested by having to work and smile through all this without the world seeing my pain. I was paddling like a duck, trying to keep everything smooth on the surface.

We had moved out of the corporate apartment, gotten our belongings out of storage and into a house in Brandon that we rented from the CEO. It was perfect: an hour from the casino and close enough to attend Jackson Academy. The furniture that once fit into a 4,000 square foot house was nestled tightly into our new, cozier home. Most of it stayed in the garage until I could give it away.

Things did not seem as important anymore. I just didn't want to spend thousands on purses and furniture that I once found pleasure in collecting. And as I got rid of material things, I found I had more space for the people in my life. Case was thriving.

By seventh grade, Case had found his home at Jackson Academy in the choral department as a member of the award-winning show choir, Showtime, and eventually Encore in high school. I was beyond comforted when Case told me that he was trying out for the show choir. At first, though, I had no earthly idea what he was talking about. In Vegas, St. Louis, and Kansas City, I had not heard of this. It surely must be a "Southern thing" I thought. Come to find out it is *very* prevalent in the South. Case practiced and practiced and practiced singing and dancing in our house for the week prior to his very first try-out for Showtime at the end of sixth grade. I really had no idea what he was doing, but he had dogged determined to make this group. Fast forward to January 2015, and the curtain opens for the first time at his first competition at Jackson Preparatory School. Out came 40 darling seventh and eighth graders singing and dancing (at the same time) like stars on a cruise ship! Little girls had "poofs to heaven" (down here the higher the poof, the closer to heaven!) and wore sparkly dresses. The young men had black suits.

How did he find this sport? I was so proud of Case for his drive to do what *he* wanted to do—to try out especially considering that his mother and father cannot sing or dance, let alone do both at the same time. Case, in his short time on this Earth, had learned so much about tenacity, extending grace, loving others and loving God, that I knew God was using his trials, our trials, for the development of his sweet, little character.

So there he was on stage dancing and singing. Case had found his "home" at Jackson Academy. For the next six years, the music and theater department became his happy place. Case found he loved theater, too, and was a cast member in numerous plays and musicals. My heart was beyond happy seeing him thrive, safely, in a world that was once hurtful and harsh to him.

Work at the casino was pleasurable but more difficult than any other job I have ever had. The resort employed more than 2,000 employees. During summer months, it grew by a few hundred to staff the enormous Geyser Falls Water Park.

I was responsible for all the non-gaming operations departments: the hotel, water park, food and beverage operations, security, facilities, retail, spa, sales, and catering. Somehow, I was even in charge of an Exxon gas station. It was a learning experience to oversee a water park and gas station, but those teams already had the institutional knowledge and support to be successful.

The work was hard, but not because of the number of departments or employees—my time as vice president for Harrah's, Caesar's, and Pinnacle Entertainment had prepared me for leading large numbers of people. It was hard because trust within Pearl River had been eroded at every level. For years, leaders had been taking advantage of the casino and the employees they were supposed to serve.

Employees were lied to. Leaders had made decisions to support the casino that came at the expense of employees and the Tribe. It was heartbreaking. The stories of how leaders took advantage of the people they were paid to protect were numerous and shocking. I personally saw casino contracts that were written for services that a good leader would never approve. They were driven by pure greed. Out of the gate, trust is *always* required for a leadership position. At the resort, it took longer than usual for me to establish trust with my employees. For those who had been hurt too many times, my best would never be enough.

Employees rightfully knew that it was a matter of time before the next leader left. In their experience, leaders came and went. They just had to wait it out. I never wanted more for a group of people than I did at Pearl River Resort. I wanted my employees, their families, and the Tribe to see that trust and authenticity exist, and that they could count on me and one another. But the only person I could control was myself.

Over the next two years, the seven members of the entirely new executive team would work to improve operations and help the Chief, the board, and the Tribe secure funding for a multi-million dollar renovation that would reopen the Golden Moon casino and hotel and raise capital funding for new slot machines—the key to revenue. The bond rating for the casino was upgraded, which helped with funding. The casino was getting a much-needed infusion of capital to keep it competitive. The keys to the redesign, besides the casino product, were marketing and, most importantly, the employees.

The Chief and the CEO invested in training, which has always been my passion. The CEO brought in talented consultants from Las Vegas and started a great training program that would reach employees at every level. Most of the employees loved it.

As with any casino, some of the employees were just there for the paycheck, which infuriated me. But for the most part, people just needed to be taught how to lead. I created and led a "Leadership Learning Series" class for the director and my colleagues. Pearl River had some of the best employees I had ever worked with—they just needed their leaders and supervisors to invest in them and get on the same page about what good leadership really was. They needed their leaders to spend time and show them that people cared about them and wanted them to grow.

As time passed in Mississippi, I was becoming accustomed to the lingo, verbiage, and way of life. Having moved around the Midwest and the West, I was used to cultural change. But now that I'd moved to the South, I found there was a "whole lot of learning to be had."

Back when I lived in St. Louis, the first question people asked was, "What high school did you go to?" I'd tell them I was from Kansas, and the conversation would dwindle. In Vegas, where most people had moved there from somewhere else, the intro question was, "Where did you move from?" But in Mississippi, I was getting used to hearing the phrase, "You're not from around here, are you?"

Everywhere I went in Mississippi, my new neighbors started to show me the ropes. Take Mrs. Amanda Lick, my crazy, beautiful hairstylist who looked like Carrie Underwood. Her accent and her laugh added to her beauty. The first time I met her, she was shocked to see I was a woman when I showed up for my appointment. She'd been expecting "Don."

We hit it off immediately. When she told me early on that she was going hunting, I was stunned. "What? You're Carrie Underwood mixed with a little Carol Burnett and a twang." But Amanda taught me that tree stands and hunting camps are popular down here for *everybody.* Just like the guys, girls wipe a lot of blood on their face after a kill. I was familiar with hunting; I had taken hunter's safety with my dad so I could drive the car up and down the fields to sit in a duck blind or go pheasant hunting. But I certainly hadn't been out there wiping blood on my face.

Amanda and Mrs. Cheryl, our amazing live-in nanny, shed a light on Southern living in short order. My conversations with Mrs. Cheryl and Amanda on what you had to know to make it in Mississippi evolved into a presentation that I give some of my clients today.

Dawn's "Top 10 Learnings In Mississippi!"

10. Directions always include highway numbers, landmarks that are no longer there, and end with "if you reach the [insert landmark: barn, fork in the road, anything] you have gone too far!"

"Take the 471 to the 25 to the 16. You will pass the big red barn on the left and come to a stop sign where Piggly Wiggly used to be. Turn left. Keep going till you see the fork in the road. If you reach the grade school you have gone too far."

Everyone nods because they know exactly what the other person is talking about, including the missing landmarks.

9. People "carry" people places.

"I am going to carry Case to school."

The first time I heard this I wondered if Mrs. Cheryl, his nanny, had seen how big Case was. She repeated it. I asked her what she meant. Then she told me that in the South, we don't "drive" or "walk" people places, we carry them!

8. People "crank" cars.

"I am going to go out and crank the car," really means they're going out to start it. Reminds me of the Waltons.

7. People use words all the time that are not in the dictionary.

"It's a real **gullywasher** out there." Gullywasher = heavy rain.

"My back is all **stove up**!" Stove up = tight.

"Mommaanthem" = just like what is looks like. My momma and them, all in one breath.

"Buggy" = shopping cart.

Just to name a few.

6. If girls have two names, you must use both names.

"My name is Anna Catherine, not just Anna." Case came home and told me this his first week in school. I giggled.

5. The "switch" is the real deal, and it is always best to pick out your own form of punishment when offered.

4. There is "y'all" and there is "all y'all."

The numbers included in each of those is hotly debated; I just know "all y'all" is a few "y'alls."

3. There are five seasons in the South.

Down here, we also have "hunting season."

2. SEC football is a religion.

Game times are to remain sacred. Do not plan weddings, events, or anything you want guests to actually attend when an SEC game is scheduled. Rivalry is real. Women dress in nice clothes and represent their school right down to the color of their nails and heels. Interior decorators take care of tailgates, which include china, chandeliers, big screen TVs, floral arrangements, and the best spread of food outside the Ritz-Carlton.

1. "Bless your heart" is not good.

The first time someone said this to me at the casino, I knew I had done something really stupid. It is all in the tone.

In my seven years here, I have learned to love the people and unique beauty of Mississippi. Though people here may question you into oblivion until they get to know you, they are innately good. I am told that not many people move to Mississippi. When I was moving across the country, the moving truck driver said he moved families everywhere in the U.S., but never Mississippi. So it makes sense that people are curious why I chose their state.

The beauty, however, is that the people who *do* move to Mississippi fall in love with it. Many never leave. When telling a Mississippian that you love the Magnolia State and are glad you moved here, most say, "Don't tell too many people. We like being a secret."

Life in Mississippi eventually settled down for me and Case. Over the years, I had come to rely on our au pairs and nannies—Melissa, Franzi, Steffi, Sally, Vivi, and Julia—as members of our family. As a matter of fact, they were one of the happiest parts of our lives. I adored the love, care, and experience they brought to Case's life. Each one of them was different; perfect for our family and for Case at that particular age. God gave us Mrs. Cheryl at the exact right time in our life. Mrs. Cheryl was a kind, loving, mature, classy, stunning, well-dressed, blonde-haired, God-fearing, and Jesus-loving Southern lady that loved Case like one of her grandchildren. She knew Mississippi, the crazy weather, the people. The house was always immaculate, the clothes cleaned and folded like a German au pair. She was selfless in everything she did. Not only was she amazing with Case and our house, but she was a dear friend and a sort of personal assistant to me. Her three spunky grandkids—Kaitlyn, Max, and Charleigh—were Case's first friends. Her daughter and son-in-law, Jennifer and Bobby, were beyond kind to both of us. I trusted Mrs. Cheryl with my entire heart. And most importantly, Case loved her, and she loved him.

Along with Case, Mrs. Cheryl saw the craziness of my work. It was not the Tribe or the employees, who I loved dearly. Here, I was never off. Never. I was on the phone before I was even out of bed, on calls during my hour drive to work, and emailing every night and weekend.

It is one thing to have periods of high work volume. I was very used to that. It is another thing to have to play the game of salvaging the dignity of others (and yourself) on a near daily basis. Tears, anger, apathy, hiding, self-medication, and alcohol abuse because of a job … It's not normal and surely not healthy for employees.

I could not bring myself to let the team, the Tribe, or the casino down. I had given up my personal life, and I knew many on the team had done the same. But I had boundaries, and I knew how God wanted me, and those I associated with, to respect others. As a senior leader, it was my responsibility to help with the environment and culture. This is what I have done (and still do!) successfully all my life. I couldn't make the pain stop, but I was sure going to give it my all.

Doing the wrong thing can cost you everything. I learned that doing the right thing can cost you just as much.

Regardless, I kept going and trying. I knew that God brought me straight to Pearl River Resort and Choctaw, Mississippi, for a reason: to help our employees be their best more than just professionally, but personally. It was clear that we had to focus on employee health and wellness. Mississippi is at the top of the list when it comes to obesity. I had been obese, and I knew the pain it caused me.

At an executive meeting in the spring of 2013, our CEO spoke about her hope to provide our workers with healthy options in the employee dining room. She wanted to offer a healthier alternative to the usual fried chicken (which was delicious and could never be removed for fear of a coup). The discussion sparked the idea for a wellness event. I had done something similar at Harrah's St. Louis and was eager to make this happen at Pearl River. I proudly volunteered to spearhead the project on top of my operations work. It meant more hours at work for me, but the benefits could be life-changing if done right. I knew some of the employees just needed a jump-start to believe in themselves.

Within a few weeks, I had recruited a rock star team from across the casino to build the wellness program. The group of six was small but mighty. In no time at all, we had a holistic wellness program to introduce to our team of 2,000. Our wellness kickoff event was going to be second-to-none.

After much pre-planning and extra work on top of our day jobs in marketing, operations, HR, and finance, we held the Pearl River Resort Wellness Event. We had teased it for weeks with the promise of a chance to win prizes if people came out to see what we were up to.

The attendance was more than expected. We filled the Golden Moon with hundreds of interested casino employees and provided hospital staff to take their biometrics. We brought in vendors who discussed healthy hearts and diabetes support, representatives from local gyms, Blue Cross and Blue Shield representatives to discuss their benefits, and healthy foods made in-house. Then, we launched a weight-loss contest. We modeled it after NBC's Biggest Loser. The concept was simple: lose weight as a team or as an individual... and win. The victors would gain more than just bragging rights.

The atmosphere was electric as we called out door prizes and blasted fun music. Excited employees chatted with one another as they poured into the room. They arrived in the photo op area, where they posed in front of backdrops, and then walked over to a table for legal sign-offs. Then, for the big "official" start they headed over to get weighed behind curtains. The swell had started! Though some employees came prepared with a team ready, other teams formed on the spot. The facilities employees formed a team just to get the free t-shirt, but ended up being the team to watch during the competition. The teams and individuals weighed in, and they were off.

Momentum started building the very first week. Pearl River Resort began to provide healthy eating options in the employee dining room and in meetings. Weight Watchers was on site and ran weekly meetings, and we confidentially tracked employees' progress. When employees stepped on the scales each week, they had lost weight. More weight than my CEO or I could have ever predicted.

In the first week, Pearl River employees lost a collective 1,200 pounds. Some of the "losers" had not even intended to join the program prior to the kickoff event. My team tracked results on weigh-in boards and I sent out a weekly email recognizing top progress. Employees were bringing healthy snacks to work, and they were working out everywhere. Teams were running up and down the stairs in the casino towers. One team of ladies—"Bianca and Company"—lost weight by running down Highway 16. Bianca, Polly, Rahka, Valerie, and LaShanda ran all over Neshoba County. Employees started asking for different dressings in the cafeteria and more healthy food options. It was magical.

At the end of the first month, we had real change. Not only did employees look noticeably healthier, there were intangible changes as well. As a whole, our employees grew happier and more supportive of their coworkers on the journey. Vendors at the resort consistently mentioned the change in the mood and culture. That was success!

The most important success to me was the growth in trust. Many employees told me they never had leaders care this much about them. I loved these employees and connected with them by sharing my story about being overweight and unhealthy (with pictures). Like many of them, I came from a trying childhood.

My test was now my testimony.

The few of us on the wellness team were still working feverishly behind the scenes to keep weekly weigh-ins going at all hours for our workers who worked overnights. Being part of the workouts and motivating my employees was deeply rewarding. We decided to propose a midway celebration to the CEO. She agreed!

We brought in NBC's Biggest Loser from Season 10, Patrick House, to come in and speak to the employees about his journey on the Biggest Loser and the Ranch. Patrick is from Mississippi and connected with our employees over health challenges that he faced in the South. He shared a private workout with the leading "losers" in both the team and individual divisions, and then went out to lunch with them. Patrick showed them how to eat healthy at a buffet...which is something we all can learn from.

The Wellness Challenge continued for six more weeks and the weight loss seemed contagious. We sent an overview of our program and the success we had to NBC's Biggest Loser. Before long, we received notification that NBC was coming to Choctaw to tape us for their "At Home Challenge."

There is no way to convey the pride the resort and Tribe had gained from this feat. NBC was coming to tape us for the world to see. This came with more work—legal sign-offs and details on how to work with the network—but I was happy to do it. We decided to announce our wellness winners at the taping. The winning team was beyond excited and proud.

On August 9, 2013, NBC came to Choctaw to tape. It was a magical day. In attendance were Chief Anderson, Mississippi Governor Phil Bryant, my preacher Chip Henderson, Patrick House and his manager Angela Ladner, and a host of others. NBC interviewed our Chief, the CEO, Patrick, our Biggest Losers, and me about the journey. Everyone signed NBC's waivers, promising that they would not speak of the taping (or tape any portion of the event themselves). Before taping the event, we all gave our phones to NBC in plastic baggies. This was the real deal.

Our mighty wellness team and Angela Ladner had the event down to a tee: matching shirts for the top wellness groups and individuals, large checks, music, and speeches for our dignitaries. The ballroom was packed to share the joy! It went off without a hitch and the winners were celebrated, honored, and photographed for our story. But then we had to wait for NBC to share the Pearl River story with the world. Though everyone was bursting with excitement, none of the 2,000 employees or 10,000 people in the Tribe broke their silence. This alone was no easy feat, but it was evidence of the pride and trust we all felt.

Soon after, we found out through our relationship with Patrick that we could be guests at the finale of "The Biggest Loser" in Los Angeles. Our Chief, our CEO, our two biggest Choctaw "losers," and myself were all invited. I was most excited that two of our employees got to travel to California for the event. I brought Case along, too. He and I had watched the show together for years in Las Vegas. We knew most of the old contestants and the trainers, Jillian and Bob. I paid for him and Mrs. Cheryl to come too as a thank you for being so selfless with our family.

At the end of 2013, our CEO had learned that our "At Home Challenge" was not going to air on NBC. We were crushed because we knew our employees and our Tribe had a story to share. They *were* winners. The CEO and I talked and decided to create a commercial to air in all our markets to play during the Biggest Loser finale recapping the journey at Pearl River Resort.

The trip to Los Angeles was wonderful, but the real win was happening back home in Choctaw. Those Pearl River employees…they were the real champions! They not only lost weight but told stories of getting off meds, apnea machines, and insulin shots. Many had the health they had only dreamed of. Most of the employees told me that they had hope for their future for the first time ever. Their lives and the lives of their families were forever changed.

Life change does not have a dollar value. Hope is priceless. This investment in our employees was not only good for business, but the right thing to do. Every casino has slot machines and hotel rooms, golf courses and spas. But happy, hopeful employees are what differentiate the best companies. We had this in Choctaw.

At the ripe age of 46 years old, I had found my "Why."

Making a Difference in this World and Sharing Hope!

CHAPTER 11

God's Provision—My Southern Gentleman

O ne could definitely say that the first few years in Mississippi were rough. Even through the personal sickness of both me and Case, his bullying and adjustment to the new school, and the murder threats, I still had joy. It wasn't always easy, but I didn't blame God or curse him. I knew, and prayed mightily, that I would come out of the darkness like I had before. And this time, I had God at my side. This was very different from the way I had handled life's blows in the past. There was no longer bottles of wine, excessive eating, and extreme dieting. I wasn't surrounding myself with *things* or throwing myself into work to ignore the struggles I faced. I was handling life's blows head on, with grace and with God.

God doesn't say it is going to be easy; he says it will be worth it.

I stayed committed to my relationship with Christ. I stayed in my Bible Study, read scripture, and journaled. Case and I went to Pinelake, and I donated to church and other organizations. I stayed "plugged in." And then the blessings came.

I had dated a bit—a very little bit—in Mississippi. My focus was on work, motherhood, and managing the three-ring circus that was our lives. I had no space in my head to date while I was being threatened to be put in a body bag. I did vow to not have sexual relations with a man, among other things that I felt God asked of me.

I had met men via Match.com, and even went out with a few of them. Most were very good men, just not the right men for me. An attorney friend of mine set me up with a wonderful Christian dentist who had decided it was time to go on a date after losing his wife to cancer some years before. It was a wonderful date, but he understandably mourned his wife's loss. We sat at a reservoir, and he cried and spoke about his beautiful wife and family. I was absolutely okay with it. I believe God put me there to be his first date, to cry beside him and minister to him.

And then one day, God dropped in my lap a man who almost seemed too good to be true. It was the summer of 2014 when God brought Randy Ammons into my life.

To describe Randy Ammons is to describe a true Southern gentleman. He stands 6'3" with perfect posture, his silver hair cut in the Air Force's "high and tight" style, a big smile, and a sweet drawl that makes everyone want to hear him talk for hours. But what drew me to Randy more than anything else was learning that he is a God-fearing, Jesus-loving man. Randy is hilarious, intelligent, witty, family-loving, and full of grace.

We met at Corner Bakery in Flowood, Mississippi for our first date. I will never forget the gray-haired, well-groomed man waiting to greet me with a beautiful smile before we walked in. It was almost too good to be true. We sat at a booth for our first date and talked and talked and talked. I remember him telling me "not to hold it against him that he was from Bogue Chitto" in his sweet Southern accent. At the time, I said I had no idea what that meant. Now I know. Today I know that Bogue Chitto is a "map dot," as Tim McGraw would say, in Southern Mississippi. A Dollar General and a truck stop. Some have told me I got myself a real "country boy."

In all reality, this "country boy" served our country as a senior master sergeant and later as Chief Master Sergeant in the United States Air Force for more than three decades. When we first dated, I could not remember his title or even what he did specifically, though I knew it had to do with security forces. The first time I saw him in his uniform, we had met for lunch in Brandon. He got out of his car, and there he was—all 6'3" of him in his ABUs. It does not get any more handsome than that.

Our first date turned into a shopping event—I had to stop by Target and Academy Sports to buy birthday presents for two friends. It was such a refreshing date and I wished it could have gone on for hours. He gave me a hug and said we should talk later.

As many women know, "we should talk later" is a painful, confusing sentence. It can mean everything from "I will call you tonight" to "I will never call you again." But Randy texted me that night, and the next day we agreed to meet for coffee at Starbucks. That date then turned into dinner dates the next two nights. He brought flowers to both. On the third date, Randy bent down and gave me our first kiss. From that day on, I knew he was the one that God had saved for me all the way down here in Brandon, Mississippi. I eventually found out—through his friends and peers, but never from Randy himself—that he was a highly respected Airman. Randy had been deployed several times and received awards for his performance and service. He was "tough as nails" as a leader. And once, while deployed to Incirlik Air Base in Turkey, his thumb was nearly bitten off by a knife-wielding Kurd during a hand-to-hand fight. I can't even imagine! But even more important to me, Randy was an amazing father to his daughter Natalie Brooke, whom he loved more than life itself.

Brooke, as the family calls her, is beautiful, reserved, crazy smart, a mean flute player, and one of the best listeners I have ever met. She is her dad's mini-me. Together they have their own language, and hilarity is the backbone of their relationship. His love for her and commitment to being a great, present dad was one of the main reasons I fell in love with him. Today she attends the University of Mississippi and plays in the band. There is nothing like a fall day in Oxford watching the band warm up in the Grove, Natalie Brooke playing along on her flute, with thousands of Ole Miss fans singing the fight song.

By December, Randy and I were engaged. Now, I always said if I got married again, I would like to get married at the Ritz-Carlton Laguna Beach overlooking the ocean. Our wedding in Yazoo City was more magical than Laguna Beach. We were married on May 3, 2015 at Calvary Baptist Church by Pastor Caleb Clark. Pastor Clark (aka Chaplain Clark in the Mississippi Air National Guard) was one of Randy's besties at the 172nd Airlift Wing. The church was a small, country church with wooden benches that could probably seat 100 people. It was perfect.

And our honeymoon to Vicksburg, Mississippi, was true bliss. I was with my new husband, staying in a bed and breakfast in the same room where

General Grant slept. We spent the day at the battlegrounds that told the story of the life and death of thousands of Americans during the Civil War.

I know some of my old friends would say, "Who is this Dawn chick? Where is the girl that loved to dance with her friends to Flo Rida and hang out at cabanas at M Pool in Vegas? Where is the Dawn who shopped at The Forum Shops?"

She was still there, but she had a new inner peace that allowed her geeky, simple Kansas-living self to shine again in an "attitude of gratitude" for God giving her a second chance. I still like Flo Rida, the M Pool, and The Forum Shops though!

God not only gifted me with a loving husband and step-daughter, but other members of the amazing Ammons family. My family grew to include Randy's brother (and best friend) Roger, his talented sister Robin, his amazing brother-in-law Steve, his nieces Jess and Samantha, their kind husbands Ben and Jordan, sweet baby Maverick, and June, or "MeeMaw," his dainty, God-fearing mother who is an angel I was blessed to meet on this Earth.

Since writing this chapter, Randy's family has endured some wrenching pain. MeeMaw was diagnosed with Alzheimer's shortly after we were married. Alzheimer's is such a soul-sucking disease. The day she did not know who Randy was took my breath away. Today, she lives in a home on the other side of Jackson, where Randy and his family still go each week to visit her. Even when she doesn't know who they are, or even who she is, they go to spend time with MeeMaw. I yearn for the day this disease has a cure. My father's family suffered from Alzheimer's as well: his father, his brother Max, and now his brother Frank.

Then on June 30, 2019, Randy's younger brother, Roger, died at 55 from heart complications. He had been sick, but it was unexpected. Randy lost part of himself that day, as did the rest of his family. Even today, I pray for Randy and his family's comfort, knowing they will see Roger again and that he is no longer in pain.

Randy's family has truly accepted Case and me as their own. God was part of this gift. That I know.

Back at the resort, the focus shifted from the Wellness Program to the approved $70 million renovation. It was such a blessing for the Tribe and resort to be given the funds to renovate our hotels, open the 70,000 square foot Golden Moon casino again, redo some additional front-of-house space, and purchase much needed slot capital. This renovation meant more business, which meant more money for the Tribe and, hopefully, more businesses interested in working with the Tribe. Behind the scenes, the marketing engine was running like a gem. The workload was heavy, but with the end in mind I felt it was worthwhile. The wellness team and I still continued with an "At Home Challenge" and even a "Biggest Loser 2" that grew to add the 10,000 people in the Tribe into our wellness and weight loss competition.

We all knew that employee health and wellness should remain a focus for the leadership team, but we did not have the bandwidth to make it a priority. Even though we had to let up on the program, there were some incredible lessons in the continuous journey towards health and wellness.

This experience was important for me personally because I found that I had no greater joy than when I was helping others believe in themselves. All business leaders know that happy employees lead to better guest service and ultimately to better financials, but I was finding that helping employees be their best personally and professionally was the key to true leadership. Wellness shouldn't just be an initiative or program; it should be part of the company's DNA.

It seemed like the resort was headed in the right direction. However, a handful of us knew that all was not as it seemed, through no fault of the Tribe or the work itself.

CHAPTER 12

Bullying—All the World's A Stage

"We desperately need more leaders who are committed to courageous, wholehearted leadership and are self-aware enough to lead from their hearts, rather than unevolved leaders who lead from hurt and fear."

–Brené Brown

I was standing with my husband and two dear friends, enjoying the private evening event that had taken over the casino floor. The room was full of energy—guests were dressed in beautiful dresses and suits, the bright lights were pulsating, and the music and sounds of slot machines filled the air. Out of nowhere the boss cut through like a whirling dervish, loud and furious. Something was not right, and I was the recipient of the leader's wrath, and not for the first time. That night's problem was not even a "life or death" issue like employee or customer safety. It was actually quite trivial, but the boss wanted it fixed *now*. My husband and my friends (who are themselves executives), stared at me in shock. The boss did not pull me off to the side to discuss, but unleashed publicly as if my guests were not valued.

I apologized, excused myself, and said I would find them later. Off I went to solve the latest in a long list of innocuous problems that could be fixed by simply asking a peer.

The hardest part about working for this leader was not even when they yelled at me, but when they yelled at others, or even worse, when they would tell me (as if they were proud) that they were going to give another executive the "silent treatment." And the silent treatment could last anywhere from an hour to a few days. Those getting the treatment knew they were on the receiving end of the "long arm of the law." Sometimes it was a blessing to not interact with the boss, but most of the time, being invisible was painful. God did not make us so we could be invisible.

 "Never let someone make you something you are not."

-Dawn Ammons

I have never understood the need for a human being to bully, berate, or intimidate another person. And it's not just limited to playgrounds and board rooms; in my 51 years on this earth, bullying has not seemed to fade away in either my personal or professional life. I talk to people every week who go through this "dance" with a narcissist or bully who drives them to tears and insanity which they take home and might even need counselors, psychiatrists, and medicine to handle. Adult bullying is not confined to the private and public business sector but is present in our schools (not just from the kids), churches, and non-profits.

Wherever it occurs, bullying is sick. As a consultant to companies large and small, and as an executive within complex, large organizations, I have seen the "best of the worst" when it comes to bullies. Mean, cruel leaders… and I laugh when I write "leaders."

The Department of Education and the CDC outline the core elements of bullying: unwanted aggressive behavior; observed or perceived power imbalance; and repetition of those behaviors or high likelihood of repetition. This includes physical, verbal, and relational harm, and the definition extends to cyberbullying. Sometimes bullying falls into criminal categories such as harassment, hazing, or assault. The statistics on the impacts of bullying on victims are astounding and include suicide. This has to stop, and it's up to me and you.

My son and I both have been on the receiving end of bullying, and it is horrific. It was worse for me when Case went through it than when I did myself (I was sure I was going to have to punch someone). But rest assured that repeated bullying can wear anyone down—as a child or an adult. I have been at the receiving end twice in my career. Those people repeatedly screamed at and belittled me and others in front of everyone like it was a normal part of the work day. More than once I hid in my office, hoping for the "all clear," just like my son did when he found the video of himself being bullied online.

I vividly remember as a senior executive, I was in a meeting with 50+ leaders all seated classroom-style in a conference room when the boss asked a question and waited for answers. After someone spoke up with an idea, the boss literally shut the person down, berating them and treating them like they were an idiot.

This made me boil inside. I was like, "What the heck" as the boss continued demeaning the more junior leader. I mustered my strength to stand up for this person who was two levels below the boss...and then I got the stink eye. But the barrage stopped for the moment. I knew it would be bad news for me later. With this boss, it just never stopped. Leaders came to me all the time to try to change how the boss was treating them, but I couldn't. The scary part was trying to figure out who was going to be the recipient of the next explosion and predicting when it was coming.

This is definitely not to say that I haven't lost my cool with my employees and the people I work with, because I have. Did I regret it? Yes! Did I apologize? I sure hope so.

Leaders, you own this in your work environment. Employees come to work to pay their bills, to learn and grow, to make a difference in this world. You are not better than any one of them. Your past trauma may make you think you have something to prove, but you don't. Get help. I know that God will sort us all out in the end, but in the interim, take your leadership position as an honor to help others be their best for them and for your company. And if nothing else motivates you, get yourself help to improve your bonus. Everyone else will also reap the benefits.

It is not okay to bully, ever. Yelling and screaming at your employees is wrong. The silent treatment—ignoring them in meetings, in the hallway, or even purposely not answering emails—is equally wrong. Top executives want great cultures, but the truth of great cultures (and a safe environment) is how executives handle *every* employee (including those at the top, good and not-so-good employees). If the top, top, top person is the bully, then I always recommend that the employee leave. It is the day-to-day conversations which determines your culture and your bottom line—not some fancy values sign on the wall.

Whether it was when I was in middle school and the girls were laughing at me in my Olivia Newton John workout headband, or when I was in my 40s and 50s and hiding from my boss at work, my experience with bullying has always been *painful*. Research shows that emotional harm feels like physical harm for youth and adults. The brain interprets much of this mental abuse in the same manner as physical abuse. The number of executives and employees I knew who were taking Xanax because of bullies and an unsafe workplace is sad. One friend kept Xanax in their desk at all times, and another friend took the top dosage of Xanax to get through the work day.

There is not enough money in the world (or a job valuable enough) to work in a toxic environment. The statistics on bullying in the workplace are only growing. Luckily, you can spot a toxic environment in a New York minute: a boss, or sometimes two, lead the conversation. Actually, they are the only ones who speak. The others in the meeting nod their head or sit quietly. No decisions are made, just agreement of the bully boss's "always brilliant" idea. And if you do disagree—Lord help you. You're about to be shut down. Yet these "leaders" in the business world think they are doing the best for the company (being the only smart one in the room), when in truth they are *taking* from the bottom line.

Employees have eight+ hours in a day. When employees work for amazing leaders, the sky is the limit. Their productivity soars and they give their heart to the company. When a bully leads, the employee does enough to get by and then runs screaming for their car at the end of the day.

My prayer is that one or two bullies read these words and stop inflicting pain on others. "Hurt people…hurt people," and it needs to stop.

 "Speak up for those who cannot speak for themselves."
(Proverbs 31:8)

CHAPTER 13

"You Gotta Know When to Fold 'Em."

I am an overcomer by every definition of the word. I have survived loss, poverty, addiction, my child's sickness and bullying problem, death threats, and so much more. No amount of money could keep me at a job that was killing me inside.

Work is never worth your sanity. I found myself angry, exhausted, and sick. Whereas when I was younger (before I had a relationship with Christ) I might have stuck out the work and ignored my pain, this time I knew it was time for me to leave. I was ready.

In June 2015, I resigned. I walked out of a meeting, grabbed my stuff from my office, and went out the back door. At home, I wrote a resignation letter and left the more than $200,000 salary (and that's not including the bonus) behind. All my cards were on the table. Some could say I lost the hand, but those who know me—those who know what *really* matters—would say I won that day. *I* believe I won the hand back in May 2009 when I gave myself to Christ.

Case, who was 13 at the time, had watched the utter insanity from a distance for nearly three years and served as my ultimate wake-up call. His comments and reactions showed me that I was no longer the mother or businesswoman God created me to be. As much as I tried to hide in the aisles of Target or in a corner of my house when I took work calls, every time I finished talking sweet Case would look at me with sadness in his eyes. "You okay, Mom?"

Leaving this job did not come without months and months of conversation after conversation, text after text, and email after email. I loved the Tribe, my team, the casino, and the employees, and the thought of leaving them saddened me. But I also had boundaries now, and I valued the team, my family, and myself more than I loved the money or the job title. With that, it was time for me to go. Doing the right thing sometimes means standing alone.

And so I left.

I soon found out that employees on all levels were told they could lose their job for reaching out to me. Some thought I had cancer or worse. Within a few weeks I started to receive texts. One person wrote, "Don't tell anyone I am texting you. We have been told more than once not to contact you, but are you okay?" Who tells employees this? I was overwhelmed with tears.

It was over and I was done, but I couldn't stop crying.

I would soon find that I was grieving the job I loved. After I read *On Death and Dying* by Elisabeth Kübler-Ross and David Kessler, I realized I was going through all the stages of grief: denial, anger, bargaining, depression, and acceptance. Some stages longer than others. This is not the first time in my life that I had been grieving like this. The difference *now* was that I had placed God and Jesus first in my life, and I had the support of my church, bible study ladies, and husband. I had bountiful hope, but I was still all over the board with crying, anger, and even depression. As Kübler-Ross writes, there is no exact order for the stages of grief, and the continuum is not linear. Grieving just happens.

I flat out missed the Tribe, the employees, and the ability to make a difference in a world I could offer help and hope.

 "Fight the good fight of faith. Take hold of eternal life to which you were called and about which you made a good confession in the presence of many witnesses."

(1 Timothy 6:12)

I eventually found a new and better self with the support of an amazing husband, brother, and group of friends.

One day, my two sweet friends from Bible Study, Jennifer Van Norman and Julie Ethridge (the VP of Bible study operations, communications, and transportation) rolled into my driveway after I missed a Bible study. They knew I was sad and isolating myself because I didn't want people feeling sorry for me. Julie and Jennifer whipped open their Bibles, and there we sat. The Bible study in my living room that day was filled with tears and prayers. Those ladies loved me when I hurt the most. I was reminded that God had delivered me from much worse in my life, and that I would not only survive but come back stronger.

I am not good at sitting back and feeling sorry for myself, so I got right to work on using my "Why" to figure out which way to head for the next steps in my career. While I had saved some money, I had a child in private school to support and a new family. I did not want to burden anyone. Time was a factor when it came to finding my next source of income, but I didn't want to rush into the wrong thing.

Each day, I sat in my home office and pounded away on my computer in two directions. The first direction was more familiar: a VP job in the HR or casino world near home. The second direction felt more daring: I began building a business plan for a new venture. I wanted to develop a company that could help corporations build successful health and wellness programs for their employees. The differentiator in my company was my focus on the "health" of the leaders at the top. Those are the people who can make employees personally and professionally better (or those who don't and instead add to the company's wellness woes). Each day, I clipped along at contacting old business friends and sending out resumes all while building my business plan and doing research—lots of it.

During this time, I discovered a few gifts I didn't know I had, like cooking. Everyone who knows me knows that cooking is not my sweet spot. Sure, I could make homemade chicken pot pie from the Hungry Girl cookbook, a simple waffle, and a perfect cup of coffee. It was not that I couldn't cook, I just never had time. But now, I found joy in trying to make a good meal: air fryer chicken nuggets, salmon, and homemade chicken salad with grapes and walnuts and much more. I enjoyed making dinner for my family. Another upside to my newfound free time was that I got to be a "carpool" mom, which I *loved*. It gave me the chance to visit with Case on our drives to and from Jackson Academy. From kindergarten to seventh grade, from Las Vegas to Jackson, I could count on my hands the times that I was able to either take Case to school or pick him up. But now I could do both. What a blessing it was to talk, laugh, sing, and even just sit while he studied on the way to Jackson Academy.

I even found joy in cleaning my own house. It was spick and span and cleaned appropriately thanks to my executive housekeeper experience. (Only when my business got crazy busy did I turn the cleaning over to our lifesaver housekeeper, Amy.) I also started volunteering at Jackson Academy. I was the chairman and co-chair of the Jackson Academy Show Choir Invitational for four years. It was only supposed to be a two-year stint according to my buddy and fellow co-chair, Charlotte McClellan, but I signed up until Case's graduation. What a gift, though, to share Case's greatest passion of show choir with him! God truly blessed me with more than I could have ever prayed for. Because I walked away from my job, I was able to participate in the "small stuff," which is really "the big stuff."

CHAPTER 14

Going All In!

In October 2015, four months after leaving the resort, I officially founded Going All In, LLC. My company launched as a health and wellness company because I wanted to share my learning and successes from Pearl River Resort and my 20+ years of leadership with other companies in this space. Not to mention sharing the successes and failures of my own journey with physical, mental, and spiritual wellness.

I chose the name "Going All In" as a reference to the casino world. When a poker player bets everything they have on one hand, they "go all in." Likewise, I was "going all in" to help make a difference in the lives of others! It seemed like the natural name for my company.

"The health of your company is determined by the hearts of your company."

– Dawn Ammons

Out of the gate, starting your own company is terrifying (but not as scary as not working at all). I spent hours sitting in my home office staring at my computer, trying to figure out what I needed to do *first*. I had to have a logo and business cards, but nothing was more important than a plan. That would be enough to get me up and running, I thought. I probably needed a presentation too, so I had friends help me with that. And off I went. I made calls day after day after day to friends and leaders I had worked with, people who trusted me. I made calls until my ear hurt from being pressed into the receiver and sent emails until my hands cramped. I heard "no" and "not now" more than "yes, let's talk," but I believed in my work. I wanted to empower companies to help their employees with their lives.

Then came my first work with Angela Ladner, one of my besties and the manager of Patrick House, the Biggest Loser who'd come to the resort to help with the wellness evens. Angela is *the* consummate Southern Lady. Her Southern accent is polished and firm; her laugh is as big as her brown eyes. She has impeccable manners and her thank you notes arrive on time. Angela was the perfect introduction to Mississippi, and my first dear friend when I arrived. She has taught me what I know about being a lady in the South. From her I learned how to cook, what to wear to SEC football games, how to host the proper "tailgate" in The Grove, and the proper use of the word "bless." Angela taught me that Mississippi storms "come in from Vicksburg." I love her like a sister.

Angela found Going All In's first client. I followed her to Vicksburg to help her buddy Rowdy Nosser with his restaurant. My part was merely to discuss customer service with the team. I loved being back in the saddle, even if only for a couple hours. My time was supposed to be free, but Rowdy, one of the funniest, kindest Southern gentlemen, handed me an envelope with $160 cash in it, the first money for my new company. I had revenue. That was *the best* $160 I had ever made! I went home and handed the envelope to Randy and he just smiled. Sweet Angela is still part of my life each day, but Rowdy passed away too early from a stroke at age 55 in 2017. I will always thank Rowdy for the role he played in my story.

Then a business friend, Larry Guillory, took a chance on me. I had worked with Larry in Las Vegas at Harrah's in the corporate offices. We knew each other's leadership style, quality of work, and sense of humor. Larry was the Chief Administration Officer at Emerus Holdings (the leading developer of micro-hospitals across the United States), and the company was interested in beta testing an employee wellness program. I flew to The Woodlands, Texas and presented my work, my company, and my plans to Larry and a team of ER physicians and senior executives. It was a go!

At Emerus, God led me to a young lady who would forever change my life. Brittany Smith was their manager of employee experience and did everything HR. Together we were the "juice" behind the wellness program. Brittany is

20 years my junior. I know it was God who put us to work as partners and eventually the best of friends. Brittany is technically a millennial, but she is everything a millennial stereotype is not. On top of her work ethic, she is crazy tech-savvy and wants her work to make a difference. Brittany is my funny, driven, intelligent, God-fearing, Jesus-loving, people-loving friend who has the soul of an 80-year-old woman. Plus she's beautiful, with her bouncy black curly hair and big brown eyes. Brittany is an entrepreneurial and authentic marketing guru. You don't get much better than that! As much as Britt was the yin to my yang, she and I saw the world the same. We 100% cared about making a difference. We grew to trust each other with our whole hearts. To this day, I cannot go too long without hearing her voice.

Together, Brittany, Larry, and I built a beta wellness program for Emerus's San Antonio hospitals and their Woodlands corporate office. There's nothing like talking to healthcare employees about their health. They know more about it than I do, but the pressure of their work and the hours they kept were hurting their wellness. Over time, the "Healthy Together" program built traction. Employees were moving (the primary goal in the beginning), and they knew the importance of being healthy after staring their biometrics in the face. In time, there was not only weight loss, but beautiful stories of life change. In 2017, FitBit named Emerus a finalist for "Healthiest Employer" and for "Best Approach to Diversity and Inclusion." What an honor! What an awesome God to lead me to Larry, to Brittany, and to making a difference with their team.

I soon picked up other big accounts, but like all entrepreneurs, I learned it took a lot of people saying "no" before I heard "yes." By all accounts, I am still learning the skills of grinding, selling, and believing in your "Why." My "Why" is to make a difference in the lives of others, not work.

Then God gave me another gift unlike any other.

It was the spring of 2018, and I was working steadily in my office. I happened to be on LinkedIn to peruse what was going on with the industry and my friends. A post from someone I did not know appeared because an old coworker had liked it. The post, from a company called Goodnight & Associates, read: "We are hiring—Executive Consultant/Coach! We are looking for the best innovative, creative, and dynamic individual with a passion to help others grow and achieve success."

It went on to say that the group was looking for someone with executive presence and experience in leading and managing teams, organizational development, and strategic planning. They wanted someone who values servant leadership, was empathetic, could travel in Oklahoma and Texas, and pass a government background check. Then came the kicker, Goodnight & Associates was especially hoping for someone with tribal experience.

I remember staring at the red and black advertisement. Then I showed it to Randy and Case. I swear it was written just for me. I composed an email, attached a resume as instructed, and sent it to Dr. Karen Goodnight, the owner of the company. Then I waited. I knew this was just for me.

A couple weeks later, Dr. Goodnight emailed me, and we set up a time to talk. The talk was wonderful, and we connected on so many levels: from our work and love of family, to our goals and love of Christ. It really seemed too good to be true. In May 2018, Case and I decided to take a little road trip to Norman to meet Dr. Goodnight, spend time together, and visit the Midwest. Case and I hopped in our rental car and off we drove to Oklahoma. In 10 short hours of singing along to music to keep us going, we had made it with only three stops for food and gas. We listened to Run DMC and Tim McGraw, Chris Tomlin and Lady Gaga…and many more of Case's songs I cannot name!

Dr. Goodnight and I met at a Barnes & Noble in Norman. I arrived a little early to get my black coffee and settle in before she arrived, or so I thought. She was 10 steps ahead of me, already seated in the coffee shop with work going full speed. I sat down and felt immediately at ease. Karen's demeanor is relaxing, soft, and polished. She is a walking Brooks Brothers advertisement—crisp and stunning. More beautiful than her incredible intelligence and wisdom is her love for Christ that shows the minute you meet her.

I sat down and we talked and laughed. Karen told me her business partner, Annie, would be dropping in to say hello though she knew she would be a bit late. Karen told me I would "know" Annie the minute she arrived from her energy. And sure enough a few minutes later, from across Barnes & Noble, came the beautiful ball of energy, blonde hair, and beautiful big eyes that caught me from the moment she entered. Annie was talking to us before she ever made it to the table! The three of us sat, talked, and laughed. Karen later said that she watched Annie and me for some time. She knew it was perfect. Annie left, and Karen and I decided to work together for one of her existing clients in Oklahoma to see how our leadership styles meshed. I was so excited! Karen and I had no mutual friends, and the only reason our paths crossed is that I happened to see a LinkedIn ad liked by someone I knew. We would later know this was all God.

Case and I loaded up in the car and headed back to Mississippi. It was a long, fun day filled with laughter and a tour of Oklahoma, Arkansas, Louisiana, and Mississippi.

I waited a couple days and did not hear from Karen. I knew she was busy and traveling, but it felt odd I had not heard from her on the specifics of our first account together. I texted her and she immediately replied, "Can you talk?" I knew it wasn't good, but I had no idea how bad it was going to be. I called her and in a broken, crackly voice she said, "Annie is dead." And then there was silence.

The conversation that followed was quick and quiet. Karen went on to say that Annie had been killed by a drunk driver on June 6, on the way home from one of their accounts. Karen was crying and her words were broken. I hurt so badly for Karen and for Annie and her family. I didn't know what to say next as I sat at my desk, tears streaming down my face. I told Karen that I would pray, which was all I knew to do. Karen said she would call me later. Then I sat in my office and cried. I had just met the beautiful, joyous, life-changing Annie and she was gone. Karen was in extreme pain. I texted my ladies in Bible study and asked them to pray with me.

Some days passed and Karen texted to talk. I did not expect to work with Karen moving forward, and I was okay with that because God manages the details. I did know, though, that I wanted to be her friend and help in whatever way she needed. Karen and I talked for a while about Annie, Annie's daughter, the funeral, and how Karen was doing. Grief was not new to Karen either; she had lost four sisters, her father, and recently her mother, who was her best friend. One thing Karen knew was that she had to get back to work for her heart and in honor of Annie. So Karen and I started our journey together.

We met in Durant, Oklahoma, and that was the beginning of the amazing friendship and work partnership that God saved just for me. We tell of our "God Story" to our clients and our friends, as we know that only God could have orchestrated our meeting. Our work has been blessed beyond all measures, not just financially, but through the lives we have been able to touch…all in the glory of God.

CHAPTER 15

Your Promised Land is Waiting

I n *Developing the Leader Within*, one of my all-time favorite authors, John Maxwell, writes:

> *"Bury a person in the snows of Valley Forge, and you have George Washington. Raise him in abject poverty and you have Abraham Lincoln. Strike him down with infantile paralysis, and he becomes a Franklin D. Roosevelt. Burn him so severely that the doctors say he will never walk again, and you have a Glenn Cunningham, who set the world's one-mile record in 1934. Have him born black in a society filled with racial discrimination, and you have Booker T. Washington, a Marian Anderson, a George Washington Carver, or a Martin Luther King, Jr."*

I am no George Washington, Abraham Lincoln, Booker T. Washington, or any of the rest.

I am, however, enough.

I am enough in spite of my childhood.

I am enough in spite of what others have told me.

I am enough in spite of being broken.

I write to tell you that my journey of 51 years has been anything but easy, but it has also been beautiful. I have a life of love, peace, and meaning. My husband and two children are kind, God-fearing, and Jesus-loving. My caring friends pray for me and this world. I am blessed to be able to do work that makes a difference, even a slight one, in the lives of others. I know that God knows my heart on good days and bad. Brandon, Mississippi, was nowhere on my radar of where I wanted to live when I grew up, but God knew where

I would prosper. God knew that my "land of milk and honey" was there for my taking, I just had to have complete faith in him, alone.

I thank God for my trials because without them I never would have found him or developed a relationship with Jesus Christ.

You are also enough.

You are enough in spite of your past.

You are enough in spite of what others tell you.

You are enough in spite of being broken. Broken crayons still color.

Your story, like mine, has meaning.

This is my testimony.

My wish for you is that you find the Lord, Jesus Christ, and have a relationship with him, too. That is my gift to you.

Your Promised Land is awaiting.

All my love,

Dawn

ACKNOWLEDGMENTS

My first thank you is to my life's greatest gift, Jesus Christ, for never giving up on me. My life is 100% different with you at the helm. May the healing you give to me be the healing I share with others.

To my family.

To my best friend and husband, Randy, thank you for always supporting me in everything that I do. You have never once discouraged me from starting my own company or writing this book. You are an amazing husband and best friend who makes me laugh every day. You are my strength in this crazy world. I love you, and I love us!

Mom, thank you for being the hardest-working, most loving, never-complaining person I know. You were always there for Max and me, and for that we will always be grateful. Thank you for being a great mom to me and a wonderful grandma to Case, helping raise him for his first five years. The memories Case has of you will live forever.

To my son Case McKinley, you have been the reason I kept going many a day. It was you and me for many years, and I never wanted to let you down. You were my strength when I had none. I am so blessed with your heart for the Lord and others! I love your zest for showchoir, hunting, fishing, skiing, Orange Theory workouts, travel, good food, and laughing with your friends. Your dad, Randy, and I are so very proud of you. You go do you and make a difference in this world!

To my brother Max. This is partly our shared story. I am glad that Mom and Dad didn't take you back to the hospital when you were born like I asked at the ripe age of 5. I cannot image sharing this journey with anyone else but you. Your passion for others, especially your family, is unmatched. Your laughter lights up the room. Mookie Boy, you will always be the #1 son.

Erika Lewy, you are the world's best editor. Unmatched. I thank my high school friend Chris Evans for recommending you. He knew exactly who I needed to bring my story to life. Your heart is beautiful. Your skills are beyond professional. I moved from telling to showing in my own slow going way, but you were "the gravel" in my story! I thank God for you all the time!

To my prayer warriors—Brittany Smith, Mitzi Cordle, Dr. Karen Goodnight, Gina Mulholland, Julie Ethridge, and Sherree Allen—thank you for always having me in your heart and praying, praying, praying for my strength, peace from God, and that my words bless others and bring them closer to Christ. I felt your prayers. There is nothing purer and more honest than a friend who prays.

To Melissa Vout, Franzi Weggner, Steffi Perko, Sally Bachman, Vivi Schloesser, Julia Grund, and Mrs. Cheryl: you are family and will always be family. Though you left your families to come live with us—most of you from the other side of the pond—I thank God all the time for the ladies he placed in our lives to love on Case with us. Each of you has a beautiful place in our hearts. I love you all and am so proud to call you each family.

To the spunky Erica Kosemund, marketing guru from Oklahoma, thank you for the title *Betting on Faith*. It took you minutes to come up with the perfect title for my memoir. You are a beautiful, crazy smart girl (with a Texas-sized smile and great makeup)! Thank you for the little smile you bring to me frequently on Snapchat and on IG. P.S. You and Jill are awesome fashion and travel bloggers. Go ladies go! #ourloveslist.

And thank you to each of you I was blessed to talk with during the editing part of the memoir. How great it was to catch up with family, high school and college friends, and incredible leaders from each chapter of my life. Reconnecting with you was the highlight at the end of writing and editing that made the process (albeit sometimes painful) freeing and worth it. Thank you all for your part in my journey.

With love and gratitude,

Dawn

ABOUT THE AUTHOR

After 20+ years and top executive roles in the casino industry—including top positions with Harrah's Entertainment, Caesar's Entertainment, and the Cosmopolitan of Las Vegas and others—Dawn Ammons is a sought-after leadership consultant, executive coach, and motivational speaker. As founder and Chief Heart Officer of Going All In Performance Group, Dawn's passion lies in inspiring people to become their best selves, personally and professionally. She works with companies to improve their teams through leadership development, training, and coaching. She is a graduate of the University of Kansas. This is her first book.

Dawn's priorities are her relationships with Jesus Christ and her family. She also enjoys working out, volunteering, strong coffee, her rescue dog Maci, and laughing. She and her husband, Randy (a 36-year veteran of the United States Air Force), live in Brandon, Mississippi, and have two adult children, Brooke and Case.

To contact Dawn for speaking or training, email her at info@goingallin. net or visit www.goingallin.net.